THE
CAMPERVAN
COOKBOOK

THE CAMPER VAN COOKBOOK

Life on 4 wheels, Cooking on 2 rings

MARTIN DOREY
RECIPES BY SARAH RANDELL

RECIPE PHOTOGRAPHS BY DAN JONES

SALTYARD BOOKS

SALT · YARD
BOOK Cº.

FOR JOANNE, MAGGIE AND CHARLIE
WHO HAVE JOINED ME ON THE BEST JOURNEY EVER.
AND
MARTIN, CATH, JACK AND THOMAS,
THE COOLEST CAMPER VAN CAMPERS OF THEM ALL.

"I'LL BE GOING WHERE I CAN IN MY BIG BLUE CAMPER VAN
AND THIS HAPPY, HAPPY FACE WILL POP UP ALL AROUND THE PLACE.
GIVE ME STRENGTH TO STAY AWAKE
FROM DAWN TILL DUSK, FROM DUSK TILL DAYBREAK."
'CAMPER VAN', The Adventure Babies.

CONTENTS

LIFE ON 4 WHEELS

What is it that makes camper van living so special? Memories of long hot summers? The idea that you can take off at any moment? Driving something that brings a smile to your face? Who knows? But what's certain is that a camper van promises freedom, fun, adventure and an escape from the everyday. It's a chance to live the dream, out in the open, away from the rat race.

Come sunset, a camper van will enable you to relax around the campfire until you're ready to turn in – because there's no need to hitch a ride home. You can just roll into bed and wake up early for the next day's adventure. Even in winter, when it's freezing outside, your home from home will give you somewhere warm and dry to brew up a cuppa.

Successful camper van living – even if it's just for a weekend – requires humour, resourcefulness and a little bit of imagination. In *The Camper Van Cookbook* you'll find everything you need to start your journey. You'll pick up a few tips on simple foraging, the rules of the road, camper van etiquette and a whole lot more besides. You'll find out how to get a warm shower in the middle of nowhere and why you should never drive in flip flops. Of course, most importantly, you'll find lots of delicious recipes to cook on your two-ringed stove.

Anyone can heat up a tin of beans, but to cook really well in a camper van, you're going to have to forget the fancy kitchen you've got at home. It's all about organising your space and using as few pots as possible. When you're settling down to an outdoor feast with the best view in the world, the last thing on your mind should be the washing-up. But that doesn't mean you can't be adventurous, which is why we've included some dishes for really special occasions. If Rick Stein can cook a fabulous dish on one ring on a boat, you can serve up a camper van banquet on dry land...

You don't even have to confine yourself to cooking inside the van – barbecues and open fires are all part of the experience. So you'll find some great recipes for those days when you don't fancy being confined to the camper van kitchen (even if it is parked at the beach). Just slide open the door, light up a fire and live a little. You're about to begin the adventure of a lifetime...

FRIDAY NIGHT

The weekend starts here

It's the end of the working week and you've got that Friday feeling. The countryside is just a short dash (and a little bit of traffic) away. But before you can park up and crack open the wine, you've got to hit the road and join the great Friday getaway. There's no time to lose.

MAKING A QUICK GETAWAY

If you're organised you'll be on the road before you can say 'wash one, wear one'. And that'll be because you've got everything – and I mean everything – you need for basic camper van survival packed up and ready to go, even down to a spare toothbrush in case your last-minute packing becomes a little too last-minute.

It's all very simple really. Keep your van in a constant state of readiness and, come Friday, your departure will be painless. To make it totally foolproof I've put together my checklist for a quick getaway. It's like a second home inventory for life on the move and means that, even if you have only a moment to dash home and change before heading off, at least you'll have the bare essentials. If the worst comes to the worst, all you'll have to do is buy a few perishables when you get there.

For me it's a psychological thing too. If the van is ready, then so am I. No matter what happens, come the end of the working day, I feel as if I can take off at any moment, even if all I can manage is a trip to the park for a brew. Keeping the van ready gives me the illusion of freedom. And that makes me feel good. Skip that late meeting! Forget the chores! I'm off.

Grab a loaf and a pint of milk from the corner shop and make a run for it

WHAT'S ON THE STEREO...

THE BEST CAMPER VAN DRIVING ALBUM EVER!!!!!!!
(Volume 23.4)

Camper Van - THE ADVENTURE BABIES

Go Mr Sunshine - REMI NICOLE

Have you fed the fish? - BADLY DRAWN BOY

Seaside - THE KOOKS

Wild Honey - THE BEACH BOYS

Free - DONAVON FRANKENREITER

Beercan - BECK

Smile - LILY ALLEN

Asleep on a Sunbeam - BELLE AND SEBASTIAN

Mr Blue Sky - ELO

Staying out for the Summer - DODGY

Lost Weekend
  - LLOYD COLE AND THE COMMOTIONS

It's raining again - SUPERTRAMP

Supersonic - OASIS

We are the road crew - MOTORHEAD

PACKING LIGHT

Packing and preparing for a trip away is very exciting. But, in case you hadn't noticed, there may be a small problem – space is very limited. Your poor old van can only carry so much. If she's creaking on her axles and bursting at the seams you've probably gone too far. How are you going to live with so little space left for yourselves? And that's before you've loaded up the bikes and the surfboards.

Any unnecessary weight will also affect the van's speed and performance. Petrol consumption will go up and the speed will go down and you can't always count on having the wind at your back. So take it all out and start again. Think to yourself "Do I really need it?" And if the answer's not absolutely yes, discard it. Unless it's the Haynes manual and the tool kit. Keep those in come what may.

I used to laugh at my Grandad when he told me stories about cutting bars of soap in half to save weight on Scout camp. But that was before I bought a VW van. Then I understood. He didn't want to carry half a hundredweight up Mount Snowdon and I don't want my van to carry half a ton of useless junk up the M4.

ESSENTIAL CAMPER VAN KIT

So here it is. The 'stuff-to-keep-in-your-van-so-that-if-you-want-to-take-off-at-a-moment's-notice-you-can' list. But not cooking kit. That's on pages 10–11.

Some things on these lists I hope you won't need – like the Haynes manual and the tool kit. But as we all know, if you forget something, you'll need it. When you're in the Outer Hebrides and it's raining and cold and all you have is a tin of baked beans to eat, where will the tin opener be? On the kitchen worktop at home, ready and waiting for someone to put it in the van, that's where. The solution to this problem: keep a spare one in the van at all times. Otherwise you'll end up trying to open tins with a rock.

ESSENTIAL KIT LIST

- ★ The Camper Van Cookbook
- ★ Cool Box
- ★ Water container with fresh water
- ★ Levelling chocks and spirit level
- ★ Folding table
- ★ Camping chairs
- ★ Sleeping bags and pillows
- ★ Toilet roll
- ★ Towels
- ★ Toothbrush
- ★ Washing-up liquid
- ★ Tea towels
- ★ Feel-good music
- ★ Maps
- ★ Haynes manual
- ★ Basic tool kit
- ★ Spare pair of pants
- ★ First aid kit
- ★ Torch or wind-up lantern
- ★ Foraging bucket
- ★ Flip flops and sun cream in case the sun comes out. You never know.

If you haven't got all this kit together, you will be able to get most of it – along with all your other vital VW camper spares – from www.justkampers.com.

TOP LOCKER AND CUBBY HOLES

The top locker is the one above the bed at the back. Most conversions will have them. They provide storage space for the more fun stuff like books, games and toys. It's the best place to put stuff that you want to take, rather than the things you have to take. A bit of frivolity.

- ★ Pack of cards
- ★ Travel Scrabble
- ★ Checkers
- ★ Dominoes
- ★ Snakes and Ladders
- ★ Books
- ★ Colouring pencils
- ★ iPod
- ★ Portable DVD player and DVDs (if you can't live without it)

Cubby holes are special places that are too small for clothes or crockery or camping hardware. They contain things you might need in the middle of the night or at a moment's notice: your Swiss army knife, a small torch, the paracetamol tablets, or perhaps an emergency bar of chocolate.

STORE CUPBOARD STAPLES

Everything is going to be fighting for space. So what should you keep in your cupboard? You'll need to be careful not to over-pack with dried food and tins you'll probably never use. However, with a few store cupboard staples on board you'll never be in a food fix and will be able to rustle up a feast in just a few minutes, wherever you are. Pasta and pesto sauce is always available in the well-stocked camper!

The list below covers the basics, but obviously you should add to or amend it to take into account your favourite ingredients. Do take a look through the recipes before you head off so that you can add anything else that you'll need.

Packing tip: it is a good idea to decant ingredients into smaller pots/freezer bags where possible to save space and weight, and then re-stock as needed between trips.

THE BARE NECESSITIES

- ★ Tea bags, a jar of coffee and UHT milk
- ★ A bottle of wine
- ★ Small bottle each of sunflower and olive oil
- ★ Tomato purée
- ★ Olives
- ★ Jar of pesto
- ★ Porridge oats
- ★ Biscuits
- ★ Peanut butter and jam
- ★ A selection of nuts and dried fruit
- ★ Dried mushrooms
- ★ Pasta, couscous and rice

TINS

- ★ Chopped tomatoes
- ★ Baked beans
- ★ Chick peas
- ★ Coconut milk
- ★ Sweetcorn
- ★ Tuna

FRESH BASICS

- ★ A few onions
- ★ A couple of lemons and/or limes
- ★ Bulb of garlic
- ★ Knob of root ginger
- ★ Chunk of Parmesan

CONDIMENTS, SEASONINGS AND SPICES

- ★ Salt and pepper
- ★ Stock cubes
- ★ Vinegar (balsamic and/or wine)
- ★ Dark soy sauce
- ★ Runny honey and/or golden syrup
- ★ Sugar
- ★ Mayonnaise
- ★ Mustard and chutney/pickle
- ★ Sauces (e.g. Tabasco, Worcestershire, Ketchup, HP, Thai sweet chilli)
- ★ Crushed dried chillies, curry paste and any other spices in the recipes you choose to cook

ESSENTIAL COOKING KIT

Many of the recipes in this book have been created using a basic set of pots, pans and utensils, so if you get to the top of Moll's Gap (and I sincerely hope you do – the views are amazing) and fancy cooking up one of our treats, you won't have to ask the people in the motorhome next door if you can borrow their zester.

Of course, if you can't live without your kitchen comforts you don't have to follow this list to the letter and you can carry all the gadgetry in your kitchen. It's your van and you can be overtaken as many times as you like.

- ★ Decent-sized frying pan
- ★ Large pan with steamer and lid. The steamer doubles as a colander
- ★ Small- and medium-sized saucepan
- ★ Large flame-proof casserole dish (or Dutch oven)
- ★ Grill for using over an open fire. Nick one from the oven at home
  – no one will miss it
- ★ Griddle
- ★ Whistling kettle. That really is camping. Water will boil more
  quickly than in a pan, saving you energy
- ★ One or two sharp knives
- ★ Chopping board or two
- ★ Grater, preferably a box grater that includes a zester on one side
- ★ One set of utensils per person (think about the weight of
  excess cutlery!)
- ★ Measuring spoons and measuring jug (useful for measuring
  dry ingredients as well as liquids)
- ★ Bowls or Tupperware boxes, big and small, for mixing and serving
- ★ Jam jar with a tightly-fitting lid
- ★ Wooden spoons and a pastry brush for brushing vegetables
  with oil on the barbecue
- ★ Vegetable peeler and a potato masher
- ★ Swiss army knife (preferably one with a corkscrew)

- ★ Tin opener (and bottle opener, if your penknife doesn't have one)
- ★ Wooden or metal skewers
- ★ One set of plates per person. Melamine is light, won't smash and feels like proper camping
- ★ Tin mugs (be careful: they aren't insulated and can burn your mitts). Very useful for banging to ward off curious bullocks
- ★ Tough plastic 'glasses' and a large plastic jug
- ★ Matches or a lighter (remember, no matches could mean no cup of tea)
- ★ Firelighters. It's cheating but I never said I was Ray Mears. Very useful as a last resort if you have no newspaper or kindling and want to light a fire
- ★ Miscellaneous useful items: tin foil, greaseproof paper, Ziploc bags, kitchen towels, clingfilm…
- ★ Washing-up bowl
- ★ Scrubbing / nail brush (for cleaning potatoes, carrots, mussels etc)
- ★ Your very best sense of humour

CHILLING IN THE VAN

A lot of camper conversions have fridges. Some run off battery power (usually the leisure battery if you have one) as well as gas. This means you can fire up the fridge on gas when you're stationary and then switch to battery power when you're on the move. Please go out and buy a carbon monoxide alarm for when you run it off gas. Better to be safe than sorry when it comes to old appliances.

Other posher fridges will work three ways. This means they can run off mains power as well as battery and gas. If you intend to park up for the night in a campsite that can supply an electric hook-up (mains electric power) these are the ones to have. It means you'll also be able to run any standard 220-volt device in the van, so it's perfect for charging up your mobile phone too.

CRAMMING IT IN

If your van has got a fridge, the chances are that it's very small. So you'll need a decent cool box, especially if you want to carry lots of food with you. As with all things there is a lot of choice here – from DIY with bagged ice or an Esky, to plug-in 12-volt coolers – but a lot of classic camper owners go for the vintage look. We have a Coleman. It's a retro-look modern cooler that will hold 50 litres of food and keep it fresh for ages. It looks cool too.

If you opt for the cool box you'll also need freezer packs. Whilst they only stay cold for a day or so on the road, you can re-freeze them at some campsites, though they may charge you. The blagger's way to do this is to take your freezer packs with you when you go to the supermarket. Bury them deep in the least popular freezer in the frozen section while you shop and pick them up on the way out. If you have the nerve, leave them overnight and pick them up the next day. Put your name on them so there's no chance of getting done for shoplifting.

Of course the sensible way would be to ask first. So if there's a small local shop close to where you're staying, nip over and check it's ok. They might even oblige.

THE TWO-RING STOVE: If you're anything like me, you'll spend most of your time on your reliable old two-ring stove when you're camper van living. Big pans might need a little negotiation and a wok could be even more precarious, but it's all about practice. And be sure you've got enough gas. If you're lucky you'll also have a grill in your van. Whoopee! Cheese on toast.

PORTABLE BURNER: I use one of these to cook fish or use the griddle because you can set it up well away from the van, and you don't want the cooking smells to linger on your upholstery. These light and handy stoves look remarkably professional yet only cost about a tenner and will pack away easily into a corner of your van. It is worth travelling with one for emergencies or for taking to the beach. The butane gas canisters do last for a while but not nearly as long as the larger gas bottle in the van – so it's best to keep it for flash-frying stinky recipes or making reviving cups of tea on five-mile hikes.

THE FIRE: The original cooking method. You can't light fires just anywhere so we've only included a few recipes for cooking over an open fire. But having said that, a grill or a fire is the best way to cook a lot of things, particularly sausages and steaks. You can also steam fish in paper or tin foil, or use a Dutch oven to create wonderful campfire casseroles, stews and pot roasts. More about that on page 140.

THE BARBECUE: I'll go into a lot more detail about barbecues later. You can do it the proper way – with real fire – or you can do it the lazy boy way – with gas. I don't use disposables because they are wasteful, so in small vans bucket barbecues are the only way to go. Remember to raise it off the ground or you'll scorch the earth. Never a good policy, in anyone's book.

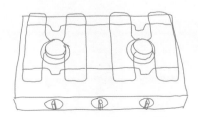

CARROTS
£1.00
£1.50
bunch

Garlic .25p each
Spring Onions 30p bunch
Cucumber 30p each
Cabbage 40p each
Beetroot 40p bunch
Potatoes £1. bag
Marrow 50p

. NEW LAID
EGGS
Doz.
½ Doz.

PICKING UP THE GROCERIES

Wherever you're heading, you'll pass supermarkets somewhere along the way, but with a little time on your side and a little adventure in your heart, you can always go somewhere different. Farm shops, farmers' markets, delis, local butchers, fishmongers, roadside stalls and local markets are the places to buy really fresh ingredients. OK so they might not have the same range of goods and the products may not be of a regulation size or shape. They may even have a bit of mud on them – but at least you'll know you're buying what's local and in season. You might even get to have a chat with the producers too. That's worth something.

I love to eat food that I have caught or sourced myself. I know where it comes from. I know no one has tampered with it. I know it hasn't been genetically modified. I know it hasn't spent weeks on a boat or truck. I know and appreciate the effort that went into catching or finding it. I know that the amount I take will have very little impact. I know it needs no packaging to sell it to me. And best of all, I know that it's going to taste absolutely delicious. That's what it's all about.

ROADSIDE ROULETTE

This is a great travelling game for people who think they can rustle up a little something out of nothing in the kitchen department. But don't panic. Roadside Roulette isn't about finding dead rabbits at the side of the road or knocking down pheasants and making a feast from the remains. It is about being resourceful.

It goes like this. In the deepest darkest countryside there may be no shops. So finding a good meal can be tricky if you passed the last Morrisons an hour ago and haven't got your foraging bucket with you. However, if you keep your eyes peeled you'll find plenty of ingredients at the side of the road – eventually. Usually it's because the locals can't get through all their home-grown veg, so rather than waste it they sell it off at little roadside stalls. You know what I mean. They are usually unmanned and will more often than not have an honesty box.

The game is simple. Nominate a chef. Stop the very next time you see anything for sale at the side of the road. Cook a meal with what you find. Condiments and seasonings are allowed. Other ingredients are not. That's the challenge. Don't forget to pay.

Sometimes you'll find a full salad just waiting to be washed, tossed and dressed, at other times it may be a few courgettes, some runner beans and an egg or two. Pray that you aren't in radish country. Either way it's more than likely that you'll be eating vegetarian when you play Roadside Roulette and you can pretty much guarantee that you'll be eating fresh as fresh can be – with as few food miles as you could ever hope for.

A couple of things to do with fresh free-range eggs bought at the side of the road

EGG TOSSING: it is a bit wasteful but it's also a lot of fun. And the better you are, the more you eat. To play you will need:

★ medium-high cliff, harbour wall or tree
★ some willing volunteers who won't sue you (or me)
★ hard hats and sunglasses

One person stands on the top of the cliff or harbour wall and throws eggs down to the others who will be standing underneath. The ones who catch their eggs intact get breakfast.

EGG AND SPOON RACES: eggs, spoons, running. It couldn't be simpler. Variations could include three-legged egg and spoon or Yummy Mummy egg and spoon (this is where one person plays the part of some royal personage at a posh boarding school sports day. Needless to say, they always win. The game is how to let them win without it looking like you let them win).

FOOD TO TAKE WITH YOU

Just because your van hasn't got an oven doesn't mean you can't enjoy a few baked luxuries while you're away. No sir! All it takes is a little forward thinking and a nice hot oven at home. Make the best of it while you've got it because once you hit the road there'll be no going back. Unless you're reading this in a fully-loaded RV with its own oven. In which case you'll be able to make these anywhere you like.

Don't forget the first rules of baking. Don't do it when you're hungry and don't let the kids eat everything before you leave. When you've set up camp and got the kettle on you'll be needing something to dunk in your cuppa.

Full-of-goodness FLAPJACKS

When you've been in heavy traffic on the M6 for a couple of hours and everyone is getting peckish, it is time to bring out the big guns. These flapjacks will do the trick. They're full of good things like apricots and seeds, but also full of naughtiness, which is what makes them so good… guaranteed to raise a smile when mid-afternoon hunger strikes. If you don't nosh the lot in one go, you can keep what's left for a few days in an airtight tin.

MAKES 16

2 TBSP PUMPKIN SEEDS AND 2 TBSP SUNFLOWER SEEDS

150G BUTTER

50G LIGHT OR DARK SOFT BROWN SUGAR

4 TBSP GOLDEN SYRUP

300G PORRIDGE OATS

2 HEAPED TBSP CHOPPED, READY-TO-EAT DRIED APRICOTS

Preheat the oven to 180°C, 160°C fan, gas 4.

Toast the seeds in a pan for about a minute then tip into a bowl to cool. In the same pan gently melt together the butter, sugar and golden syrup. Turn off the heat and stir in the oats, toasted seeds and chopped apricots, then mix well.

Tip the mixture into a lightly buttered 20cm, shallow-sided, square cake tin and press it down well with the back of a spoon. Bake for 30 minutes. Leave to cool slightly then cut into 16 squares while still warm. Once cold, remove from the tin.

GORGEOUS GRANOLA with seeds and HONEY

Granola is a wonder food. Wonder in that you could have it for breakfast and go back to the tin a little bit later and still not get fed up with it. Try it with cooked fruit for a crumble on the go. Granola is perfect for camper van living because it's light, tasty and very good for you – think of it as a very versatile trail mix. If you can't find Manuka honey, just use standard runny honey on its own.

FOR 10-12

500G JUMBO ROLLED PORRIDGE OATS

6 TBSP PUMPKIN SEEDS

4 TBSP SUNFLOWER SEEDS

3 TBSP SESAME SEEDS

2 TBSP LINSEEDS (FLAXSEEDS)

75G EACH BLANCHED ALMONDS AND BRAZIL NUTS, ROUGHLY CHOPPED

ZEST OF 2 ORANGES

8 TBSP RUNNY HONEY, IDEALLY 2 TBSP OF THIS TO BE MANUKA HONEY

100G EACH READY-TO-EAT DRIED FIGS, DRIED APRICOTS AND PITTED DATES,
   ALL CUT INTO BITE-SIZED CHUNKS

Preheat the oven to 150°C, 130°C fan, gas 2.

Tip everything apart from the honey and dried fruit into a large roasting tin. Drizzle the honey over the dry ingredients and mix everything together with a wooden spoon.

Bake for 1 hour until golden, stirring after 30 minutes and again after 45 minutes. Take the granola out of the oven, mix the dried fruit into the mixture, then leave to cool completely. The granola will become crunchy as it cools.

Store in an airtight container and don't tell anyone else you've got it on board. Eat furtively, on your own, when no one is looking.

STICKY GINGER treacle cake

This is my kind of baking. The cake takes just 15 minutes to prepare and gets better and stickier the longer you keep it (within reason). Having said that, how long is it going to last? Really?

MAKES 16 SQUARES

200ML MILK

3 TBSP BLACK TREACLE

100G BUTTER

75G PLAIN FLOUR

150G LIGHT MUSCOVADO SUGAR

50G DARK MUSCOVADO SUGAR

125G PORRIDGE OATS

4 TSP GROUND GINGER

¼ TSP GROUND CINNAMON

1 TSP BICARBONATE OF SODA

Preheat the oven to 150°C, 130°C fan, gas 2.

In a small pan, gently bring the milk to the boil with the black treacle and butter until melted. Sieve the flour into a large bowl and mix in the sugars, oats, ginger, cinnamon and bicarbonate of soda. Give the warm, melted ingredients a quick stir then mix them into the dry ingredients.

Pour the mixture into a lightly buttered 20cm, shallow-sided square cake tin. Bake for 45 minutes. When completely cold, cut the cake into 16 squares and carefully transfer them to a tin or airtight box. They may be a little crumbly but that is what makes them so good! To stop the squares from sticking together when you store them, separate them with layers of baking parchment.

Salted caramel nut SQUARES

Crikey! It's a good job you're going to be walking the coast path, going foraging in the woods and generally using up lots of energy. That's because this sweet little number is going to give it back to you, with a vengeance. Enjoy it with a brew and a view. You're on holiday.

MAKES 16

200G WHOLE BLANCHED HAZELNUTS
175G BUTTER
175G DARK MUSCOVADO OR DARK SOFT BROWN SUGAR
1 LEVEL TSP LIGHTLY CRUSHED SEA SALT FLAKES
1 X 397G TIN CONDENSED MILK
200G DARK CHOCOLATE (ABOUT 50% COCOA SOLIDS)
1 TBSP CRÈME FRAICHE OR DOUBLE CREAM

Preheat the oven to 180°C, 160°C fan, gas 4.

Toast the nuts in the oven on a baking tray for 15-20 minutes or until golden, then remove from the oven and leave to cool (you can turn the oven off now). Melt 100g of the butter in a pan.

Roughly chop the nuts, then mix with the warm melted butter and 2 rounded tbsp of the sugar. Tip the mixture into the base of a lightly buttered 20cm, shallow-sided, square cake tin and spread it out evenly with the back of a spoon. Cool, then chill for 30 minutes (or longer is fine) to allow the base to firm up.

When the base is set, gently heat the rest of the butter and the sugar in a pan with the salt, stirring all the time, until the butter has melted and the sugar has dissolved. Add the condensed milk and stir over a low heat until the mixture begins to bubble. Then boil it for 2 minutes exactly, stirring all the time. Take the pan off the heat and leave it to cool for 15 minutes.

Stir the cooled but still warm salted caramel vigorously, then pour it over the nut base and chill for another hour to set the caramel (or longer is fine). Melt the chocolate with the crème fraiche or cream in a bowl over simmering water, cool for 5 minutes, then pour over the caramel layer. Spread out evenly, then chill for 6-8 hours (or overnight) to set completely. Cut into 16 squares.

PEANUT CHERRY cookies

Chocolate, peanuts, cherries. What's not to love? Just don't tell your friends you have them on board or they'll soon be gone.

MAKES 22-24

125G SOFT BUTTER

185G CASTER SUGAR

1 MEDIUM EGG, LIGHTLY BEATEN

185G PLAIN FLOUR

2 DSP COCOA POWDER

1 TSP BAKING POWDER

100G NATURAL ROASTED PEANUTS, CHOPPED

75G DRIED SOUR CHERRIES (OR DRIED BLUEBERRIES, CRANBERRIES OR SULTANAS)

Preheat the oven to 180°C, 160°C fan, gas 4.

Using an electric hand whisk or mixer, cream the butter and sugar together in a bowl until pale, this will take 3-4 minutes. Add the egg little by little, whisking all the time. Sift in the flour, cocoa powder, baking powder and a generous pinch of salt and whisk together. Stir in the peanuts and the dried cherries.

Line two lightly oiled baking sheets with baking parchment. Bring the cookie mixture together, then form 24 walnut-sized balls. Place 12 balls on each baking sheet, keeping them spaced apart as they will spread slightly during cooking. Press down each ball lightly to flatten it a little.

Bake the cookies for 20 minutes. Transfer to wire racks to cool (don't leave them on the trays as they may stick) and then store them in an airtight tin.

23

Prune and SULTANA EARL GREY tea loaf

The great thing about this tea loaf is that it keeps well, so you'll still be able to enjoy the pleasures of home baking long after you've dropped off the dog at the kennels and cancelled the milk. It freezes too, so you could make a batch for your next trip at the same time. On the road, on a walk, on the beach, wherever. It's brilliant.

CUTS INTO 12 SLICES

100G READY-TO-EAT PITTED PRUNES

75G READY-TO-EAT DRIED APRICOTS

125G SULTANAS

100G GRANULATED SUGAR

150ML WARM EARL GREY (OR OTHER) TEA

1 LARGE EGG, LIGHTLY BEATEN

1 TBSP RUNNY HONEY

225G SELF-RAISING FLOUR

1/2 TSP GROUND CINNAMON

1 TSP GROUND MIXED SPICE

WHOLE NUTMEG, FOR GRATING

Chop the prunes and apricots, mix with the sultanas and sugar, then tip into a smallish bowl. Pour over the warm tea and leave to soak overnight.

Pre-heat the oven to 170°C, 150°C fan, gas 3. Tip the fruit mixture into a large mixing bowl, stir in the egg and honey, then sift in the flour, cinnamon, mixed spice, a generous grating of nutmeg and a pinch of salt. Mix until combined, then spoon into a lightly buttered 10 x 16cm base x 9cm deep loaf tin.

Bake for 1 hour or until the tea loaf has risen and slightly shrunk from the sides of the tin. Turn it out of the tin to cool on a wire rack. Slice thinly and spread with butter to eat.

A SANDWICH FOR THE JOURNEY

Come on, admit it. Everyone has a secret when it comes to sandwiches. Everyone has odd tastes. It could be that it's something your parents ate, that was normal in the world in which you grew up. It could be that you acquired a taste for odd combinations of ingredients during cash-strapped student days. Or it could be just that you've got odd tastes.

For me, the ultimate gastronomic sandwich masterpiece is blue cheese (the stinkier, the better), Marmite and baby spinach with mayonnaise on thick sliced crusty white bread. I know where it comes from. My friend Guy grew up on cheese and Marmite sandwiches so, when I needed a signature sandwich for myself, I stole it and created my version of it. Over the years I have carefully refined it until it has got to where it is today. Delicious.

John Montagu, the 4th Earl of Sandwich, is credited with being the 'father' of the modern sandwich. The story goes that he wanted to keep his hands grease-free during a card game so he ordered his meat between two pieces of bread. Naturally, his posh chums thought it was a jolly good idea and ordered theirs like that too. That was in 1762. The sandwich, in its many forms, has remained dear to our hearts ever since. Admittedly it would have been nicer if it had been created in battle or in a situation of huge adversity like many other great inventions. But never mind. The sandwich is easy to make, has infinite combination possibilities and is perfect for eating on the run. And that makes it perfect for us.

Of course one man's meat is another man's poison so when I started to think about sandwiches for a trip in the van, I couldn't decide what to include. I love my stinky cheese and Marmite combo, while my mum, for example, loves banana sandwiches with demerara sugar on processed brown bread. As far as I am concerned, that's not normal. But the point is, everyone has their own guilty sandwich secret.

To prove this I did a bit of very unscientific research and asked all my Facebook friends to give me their 'odd but delicious' sandwich combinations. Then I decided to make my family try them.

WHAT'S YOUR SANDWICH SECRET?

Cheese, ham, marmite, mayo and salad

Nutella and honey

Guacamole and cottage cheese with slices of tomato

Chutney, cheese, salami, tomato, gherkins, basil and mayo

Banana

Corned beef and sugar in a hot buttered toast sandwich

Cheese and beetroot

Smoked salmon, cream cheese and thin apple slices

Bacon and marmalade

Cold swede and Brussels sprouts with plenty of pepper, best on wholemeal

Cheese and strawberry jam

Gherkin and peanut butter

Crunchy peanut butter, salad cream and bean sprouts on white bread

Egg mayo, spring onion and smoked salmon

What could possibly go wrong?

Are you kidding me? Everything can go wrong here. The only way to keep safe is to make your own sarnies. That way you'll never have any reason to complain.

THE JOURNEY

Driving a classic brings its own special pleasures. Travelling in style, the freedom of the open road, going where the mood takes you. A lot of people will tell you that it's the journey that's important. So it is. But it's just as good to get there and get the kettle on. That's when you start living.

FOOT LOOSE AND FANCY FREE

One of the cornerstones of the camper van lifestyle is kicking off your shoes and feeling the sand between your toes. It's the thing that enables you to step over the line that divides you from the mainstream. Once on the barefoot side you begin to belong to the counterculture.

But hang on a second, not just yet. Keep your shoes on until you get there because if you drive in bare feet you could end up being prosecuted for driving without due care and attention. For real! And it's no good putting on a pair of flip flops either, as only appropriate footwear will do.

The result, if you get stopped and charged, could be up to 9 points on your licence, even disqualification in extreme cases, and fines up to £5,000. It's the same if you get distracted while driving: changing a CD, reading a map, smoking, eating and using your mobile phone all count. So... do the relaxing once you get there.

THE VIEW FROM HERE

When you are driving, it is worth savouring the experience. If you have far to go you're going to be doing it for a while. You couldn't hurry if you tried. You'll see more in a van because the driving position is right over the front wheels. Visibility is great. Going round sharp corners feels like floating. The whole thing is more akin to driving a truck than a saloon car yet the footprint is pretty much the same.

The other side, of course, is the feeling that something could go pop at any moment. I guess it's the same with all classics. Everything wears out at some point. You pray it's not today.

DRIVING THE ENVIRONMENTAL MESSAGE

One of the ironies of camper van culture is that it usually goes hand in hand with a love of the outdoors and a respect for the environment. Yet we're prepared to turn a blind eye to the environmental impact of our favourite mode of transport. My van, a thirsty 2.0-litre air cooled, pushes out about 15-20 miles per gallon depending on how I drive. Compared with today's standards that is very poor and perhaps a little irresponsible. Of course I could have it converted to Liquid Petroleum Gas which would reduce running costs and produce fewer emissions, but fuel economy would be worse.

There's nothing for it but to drive in a more fuel-efficient way. Here's how:

* Get your van serviced. Good maintenance will keep it running smoothly and more efficiently. There's more about this on pages 34-35.
* **Keep your weight down. Packing light is key.**
* Streamline. Ok so the shape isn't perfect but you don't need roof racks, top boxes or surfboards on the roof do you?
* Change up quickly. Get into high gear as soon as possible and don't thrash it on the way.
* Keep it smooth. Revving up uses loads of fuel so take it easy and don't push it.
* Don't idle. If you're sitting in traffic for a few minutes, switch off. It uses less fuel.
* **Check your tyre pressure. Having your tyres at the right pressure can really help to push up the miles per gallon.**
* Avoid short journeys. Short hops use more fuel. Walk or take your bike.
* Take a spare fuel can – you never know when you might need it.

MUTUAL APPRECIATION SOCIETY

There's an unwritten rule of motoring that says VW camper van owners have to wave at each other. Of course it's never simple and there are politics to it. The older vans, the Splitties and the Bays, will always offer up a friendly wave to each other but it's touch and go when it comes to the T25 (T3). Maybe it's because the T25 went water-cooled in 1982, maybe it's because they are so different from Splitties and Bays, maybe it's because they are new and therefore not to be trusted. Who knows? I suspect they're just not cool enough for the hardcore enthusiasts.

As a serial T25 owner I have become a little wary of the waving policy. It makes me feel insecure. This is probably because when I had my first T25 in 1991 they were still considered 'new fangled' by the VW community and nobody waved. Nowadays they are increasingly regarded as classics, so more and more drivers are waving. But I still feel empty and inferior if I wave at another van and they don't wave back. So I let them do the running. This is silly, isn't it? I should definitely get over myself. Who cares if they don't wave back? It's their loss.

Whoever you are, whatever you drive, share the love. Don't be aloof. We're all in it together.

SEAT BELTS IN A CAMPER

Sometimes common sense wins out. I wouldn't feel comfortable carrying any passenger in my van if I didn't have seat belts fitted. I'd feel it was my duty to get them fitted, even though current seat belt law says that if they aren't fitted you can still carry passengers in the back of a camper. But would you, knowing what you know about seat belts and impacts? I wouldn't. Not with my kids or any of my friends.

You shouldn't use seats that face the rear or side either. And don't forget that children under 3 years old cannot travel in a vehicle unless they are in a secured baby or child seat and that children under 12 must be seated in the appropriate restraints – that goes for vans too. Don't risk it. And no putting the bed out for the kids on the M25 either – no matter how tired they are.

share the love

A VERY BRIEF VW HISTORY

My van, Pootle, is a 3rd generation VW camper. Officially he is known as the VW Type 2 T3 or, in the UK, the Type 25. Unofficially he's known as 'the Brick', 'the Wedge' and sometimes as a 'bungalow on wheels', which is clearly untrue as he has an upstairs.

With looks that only an enthusiast could love, Pootle isn't the most attractive among the VW campers but the older he gets, the more he grows into himself. Being a 1981 version of the T25, Pootle has an air-cooled engine, which just about gets him in with the cool kids on the concourse. However, it won't win him any prizes as a classic. Pootle sits about halfway along the family line of the VW camper van and represents just one small (but still relevant) part of Volkswagen story.

And that begins with a famous auto engineer with an eye for style and an infamous dictator with a superiority problem...

1933 Hitler declares an interest in finding a 'people's car' for Germany

1934 Ferdinand Porsche agrees to design the people's car

1949 The first Type 2 T1 van (Splittie) is showcased at the Geneva Motor Show

1938 The Volkswagen factory at Wolfsburg is built. Hitler gets one of the first Beetles (Type 1) for his birthday

1939 War stops play – Wolfsburg builds military vehicles until it is bombed in 1945

1947 Ben Pon, a Belgian car dealer, sketches out an idea for a panel van at a meeting with VW

1945 The British forces take over the Wolfsburg factory under the charge of Major Ivan Hirst

Today… The 'Bay' is still made in Brazil. These days it has a dual fuel engine and returns almost 40 mpg. They are imported to the UK and converted into campers by Danbury

2010

1981 First water-cooled engines are fitted in the T25

2003 Production of the T4 stops in Hanover. The T5 takes over

1979 Type 3 or T25 production begins in Hanover. This is where Pootle comes in!

1982 The last air-cooled T25 is made in Germany

1979 The end of 'Bay' production in Germany. It continues in Brazil

1985 The Syncro – a 4x4 version – is introduced

1997 The last Beetle is made in Brazil

1975 The last splittie is made in Brazil

1990 The last T25 is built in Germany. The T4, the first van to have a front-mounted engine, arrives

1973 The Bay gets a revamp and is refined with bigger engine and better brakes

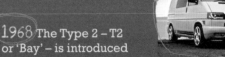

1968 The Type 2 – T2 or 'Bay' – is introduced

1950 The first Type 2 panel vans and microbuses leaves the factory at Wolfsburg

1967 The last splittie is made in Hanover. Over 1,470,000 have been made. Production continues in Brazil

1956 Production of the VW vans moves to Hanover

1951 Westfalia, official coachworks company to VW, converts its first camper model

1964 The first sliding side doors are introduced as an option

HIRING A VW CAMPER

If you don't already own a camper then the next best thing is to rent one. There are companies all over the UK and Europe where you can hire a classic split-screen camper, an all-singing, all-dancing T5 California and everything in between. So if you want to set off on your very own camper van adventure or if you are going to a festival and can't face slumming it again, or want to try before you buy, this is the way to do it. You get all of the fun, freedom and frolics, and none of the cost, worry or responsibility of ownership. All in all it sounds perfect.

What's brilliant about hiring is that you don't have to set out from your home base and face a long drive to your destination. You can simply hop on a train or even a plane and pick up your van right where you intend to take it. For visiting places like the Western Isles, going surfing in Newquay or taking off for a week in Ireland, it really is very handy. Some of the hire companies will also do a spot of shopping for you and provide a hamper for your first day or so in the wild. All you do is turn up. And if the worst comes to the worst and the beloved van gives up on you, they'll sort it out pronto as well.

Need a ride? Look no further than the directory on page 270.

GIVE YOUR VAN A LITTLE LOVE

The chances are, that if you have a VW camper that you'll bestow love, affection – and plenty of cash – on it. And so you should.

To their credit, air-cooled engines are very simple and reliable, with uncomplicated electronics. That's probably why there are so many of them around today. Even so, they do have problems and still need to be maintained properly. The more you look after your van, the more it will look after you. That's the simple message Ian at South West VWs told me when I went in search of his sage advice. Make friends with a good mechanic, he said. Older vehicles, unlike newer cars, were never designed to run for long periods without care. Service intervals are shorter.

Unless you are lucky enough to have a van that has had a complete restoration, there is bound to be some rust lurking somewhere. It might also be worth investing in protecting your vehicle with waxoyl. This will help to keep the inevitable rust at bay and will prolong the useful life of your favourite machine. Nobody wants their van to turn into a play house before its time is done.

As well as keeping your van maintained, Ian recommends that you should always carry your roadside recovery card wherever you go. Older vehicles have old parts that wear out. So be prepared.

In the meantime, there are some things to remember:

★ If either the oil or battery lights come on when you are driving, stop immediately. You could be about to boil your engine. And that isn't good news.

★ **The oil pressure light coming on means you have a lack of oil, therefore a lack of lubrication and, to a certain extent, cooling. Your engine could seize.**

★ The battery light could mean that the alternator has stopped working, which isn't serious, but because the alternator is attached to the fan belt on air-cooled vans it could mean that the fan has stopped working. Your engine could be about to overheat. And that means disaster. Better to pull over and call the specialists.

★ **Make your mechanic your new best friend. Regular servicing at 5,000-6,000 mile intervals by a good mechanic should keep your van running smoothly.**

★ An MOT is a basic test. Just because your van has an MOT it doesn't mean to say that it is reliable or a quality vehicle. All a vehicle has to do to pass an MOT is pass on the ramp. It doesn't have to be reliable, rust-free, running properly or have that much left in its brakes. Be warned.

★ Check your oil level regularly. VW engines can have leaks, which mean low oil levels, which, in turn, could mean… a catastrophe waiting to happen. No one likes a seized engine.

★ Keep a basic kit of spares and learn how to use them.

★ **Check your brake fluid. Nothing more needs to be said here really.**

★ Keep your tyres at the correct pressure. This will help to keep your miles per gallon up (see page 29 for more about fuel economy).

★ **Join a motoring organisation. 'Nuff said. And remember to get the kettle on for a welcome cuppa when they turn up to rescue you.**

A FEW THINGS TO TAKE WITH YOU WHEN YOU GO

It will help enormously if you learn how to fix a few basic common faults. Admittedly it's easier said than done, but if you can't fix it yourself at least you'll have the parts for the AA man when he turns up.

* ★ AA card (or similar)
* ★ Fan belt
* ★ Accelerator cable
* ★ Clutch cable
* ★ Points
* ★ Condenser
* ★ Spark plugs
* ★ Jack and wheel brace
* ★ Spare bulbs and fuses

YOUR NEW BEST FRIEND

If you are out and about in your van, it might help to know where to find a friendly VW mechanic. So we've listed a few on page 271. Some we know and trust, some we don't know and therefore can't vouch for. As a result it is simply a list, rather than a personal recommendation. So talk to a few van people. Get their recommendations. And just be sensible, as you would be with any older vehicle.

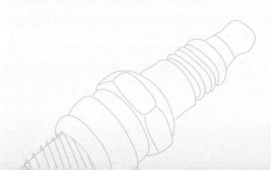

TRAVELLING WITH KIDS

If you've got a long journey, travelling with kids can take an age. Wee stops, boredom, car sickness, fighting... it all goes on. So anything you can do to keep them entertained will help. My friend Damian gave me a 'Backseat Bingo' game (see page 40). He's someone who has travelled extensively with three children so he knows his onions. Photocopy it, give one to each of the children you are travelling with and get them to fill it in. The one who fills it in first is the winner. Hours of fun.

MORE TRAVELLING GAMES

CLOUD SHAPES

Is that a bird or a dog with a bone in its mouth or is it a rabbit jumping over a rainbow? You decide. That's the great thing about looking for shapes in the clouds. They can be anything you want. The difficult part is getting anyone else to see it too. But maybe that's the point? You see what you want to see. Just make sure that the driver sees the road ahead. Strictly passengers only. Can also be played at camp.

GUESS THE ANIMAL

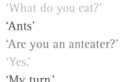

Our kids Maggie and Charlie are excellent at this. They have had lots of practice because we play it at almost every mealtime. One person has to think of an animal. Everyone else has to ask questions such as 'where do you live?', 'what do you eat?', 'do you have feathers or fur?' and the thinker has to answer as truthfully as they can. The one who guesses the animal first wins and gets to think of the next animal.

'What do you eat?'
'Ants'
'Are you an anteater?'
'Yes.'
'My turn.'
Etcetera.

EDDIE SPOTTING

This is the motorway equivalent of train spotting. Are we in that much trouble? If you've got far to go, you might just be. The game goes like this:

Each lorry belonging to Eddie Stobart hauliers has a different girl's name painted on the front of the cab. Are they the names of Eddie's previous lovers or the names of his children? Who knows. But the game is to collect them. Download a list from any number of seriously geeky websites and then tick off the lorries you spot.

PUB CRICKET

This game is easy to play and, much like real cricket, it can keep you going for hours. It's been around for years, played by generations of passengers and drivers desperate to distract their charges from travel boredom. We used to love playing it on the long journeys to Granny's house. In a van, where speeds rarely reach the dizzying heights of seventy miles an hour, it really comes into its own.

Pub cricket only works if you're travelling on minor roads as the likelihood of passing a pub on the motorway is very slim. Take turns 'batting'. When it's your turn to bat you have to count the legs of the first pub you pass. That's your score. Think about it. 'The Bull' scores four runs. 'The One Legged Pirate' scores one run, three if he has a parrot, two if the parrot also has just one leg. And so on. You are out when your pub has 'Head' or 'Arms' in the name, then it's the next person's turn to bat and try to clock up some runs. There are opportunities for massive scores in this game, especially if you pass a pub with a name like 'The Coach & Horses' (how many horses, how many legs – how many runs?), The Oval (try working that one out) or The Men of Kent (who knows?). The Douglas Bader, naturally, scores nil.

I-SPY

When times are tough and you've listened to all the CDs and played all the other van games you can think of, the passengers are still going to need entertaining. Keep this one up your sleeve and you'll see why it's been loved by drivers throughout the history of the camper van. At the right time it can be the perfect tonic.

If you've got no kids travelling with you why not try 'Rude I-Spy'? It's much like the original but with lots more Fs, Bs and Cs and a lot fewer Ps and Qs.

PITCHING CAMP

One of the best things about camper vans is that you can sleep where you park. Brilliant! Drive, kip, drive, kip, drive, kip. The possibilities are endless and finding somewhere great to wake up in the morning is half the fun. A view is ideal, seclusion is nice and security is paramount – whether you are stopping off halfway, going feral, checking in to a big site for the weekend or touring for months on end.

FINDING A GOOD HALFWAY HOUSE

If you're going far then at some point you're more than likely to want to find somewhere for a snooze. It could be a good idea to plan a bit in advance.

LAYBYS: If you park up in a layby then you could get done for obstruction. However, if you're dead beat and need to sleep before safely continuing your journey, the police will probably leave you be – unless you're parked somewhere stupidly dangerous.

CAR PARKS: These are usually governed by local by-laws, which means the rules about overnight parking will be different wherever you go. But it does mean that they are governed by civil, not criminal, law. The authority can slap parking tickets on you or get court injunctions against you.

PRIVATE LAND: If you have the nerve to knock on doors and ask people to park up on their land for the night then this is an easy solution. Some farmers and pub landlords will also let you stay overnight in their fields or in their car parks, even if they don't have a caravan site licence.

TRUCK STOPS: If it is absolutely necessary you can park at truck stops overnight. Choose your parking spot carefully. Lorry drivers may want to leave at odd hours and won't take too kindly to you blocking their way. They are unlikely to wait until you wake up to ask you to move.

MOTORWAY SERVICES: Sometimes this is the only option on long journeys. Just remember to check the parking time limits and buy a ticket if you exceed the allowed free time.

FOLLOW THE SIGNS: Wherever you see signs that say 'no overnight parking' there is a good reason for it. Be prepared to be moved on if you don't have permission.

MOTORHOME STOPOVERS: If you've ever travelled in Europe you'll know that many countries offer *Aires de Service* where camper vans and motorhomes may stay overnight. They often provide fresh water, toilets and somewhere to unload the unmentionables. You can check online for UK council-owned car parks that are authorised for overnight parking before you leave home. Try www.ukmotorhomes.net or www.motorcaravanning.com.

42

HAVE YOU PAID AND DISPLAYED?

ONE FOR THE ROAD

No one in their right mind is going to condone drinking and driving under any circumstances. Remember if you're going to be driving in the morning then take it easy the night before. Your body will take a while to process alcohol – roughly an hour per unit – so you may still be over the limit.

SLEEPING IT OFF

It's worth remembering that whenever you are in a vehicle in a public place, you could be considered to be technically in charge of it – so skip that glass of wine over dinner. You may still be drunk in charge.

Public places include car parks, so pub car parks may also be considered public spaces. Some people argue that after hours they are no longer public. But if you are kipping in a pub car park with the permission of the landlord after having had a skinful, be aware of the risks. What's more important, your licence or a couple of beers?

YOUR FINAL DESTINATION

Some people like to know where they are going and will book a campsite well in advance. Others don't, and will simply stay where they feel like once they get to where they are going. Either way it's up to you. If you trust to luck you might get very lucky. On the other hand you might not.

WILD CAMPING

Wild camping is what camper vans were made for, isn't it? Unfortunately, in England and Wales it is illegal. Sadly you just can't pitch up where you like. Every bit of our lovely homeland is owned by somebody, so you need to get their permission first.

However, as a surfer I've taken a few chances over the years so that I could wake up to the sound of the waves, so I know that there are places where wild camping is tolerated. As long as you behave properly no one will bother you. Just remember to be respectful, leave no litter and if you get asked to move on, do it gracefully.

In Scotland wild camping (with tents) is legal under the Land Reform Act 2003. The same applies to your camper van, although the usual rules apply. If you park near buildings, ask permission. Be respectful. Take your and others' litter home.

CAMPING ON CAMPSITES

If you like booking in advance, campsites are the way to go. There are literally thousands of them and there are just as many websites and books to show you the way. *Cool Camping* is the book that caught our imagination because the sites are hand-picked and among the best. It's worth the investment.

Failing that, try a few of our, our families' and our friends' favourites (listed on page 272) but please don't all rush at once.

THE CAMPING AND CARAVANNING CLUB

Every so often you need to have a hot shower, dry your clothes, spend a little time in the company of a proper loo and charge up your mobile. Many of the Camping and Caravanning Club's sites are for members only but others are open to anyone. They also have Certificated Club Sites. These are smaller, privately owned sites which are often in out-of-the-way places. They are usually somewhere remote or quiet. Sounds good? They are as close to wild as you can get without going feral. And the only way to get on to them is to join.

Check out www.campingandcaravanningclub.co.uk for details.

ONE LAST THING
...MAKE SURE YOU ARE ON THE LEVEL

There is one item that can make all the difference to your night's sleep wherever you end up: levelling chocks. They are on the list of essentials for good reason. If you have to park on a slope, your chocks will enable you to level off and sleep without finding yourself in a heap at the end of the bed in the morning.

What Could Possibly Go Wrong?
Unless things go very badly wrong you can't get in too much trouble.
It all depends on what kind of person you are. Wild and free?
Take your chances. You might get moved on, you might score. Like order and itineraries? Book ahead and avoid all the things you fear.

JGU
335C

SATURDAY MORNING

Up with the larks

After a long drive, a few moments of golden sunset on Friday night (if you're lucky) and a desperate dash for last orders at the local pub, you wake up early on Saturday morning. The first light of a beautiful new day is creeping through the gaps in the curtains. Enjoy the moment. Any minute now you are going to open the curtains and look out on your new location.

NOTHING BUT THE WEEKEND AHEAD

What will you find? If you parked up at the side of the road to get a few hours' kip before carrying on, you might well look out over concrete and Tarmac, but if you successfully reached your destination you could well be facing open fields, a beach with perfect surf, a river with rapids to race or a mountain with impossibly steep faces to climb. I once woke up in a field on a summer's morning to find a herd of cows licking every inch of my van. Literally. They like the salt from the road apparently.

Whatever you find on the outside (let's hope it's sunshine) you now have a whole day ahead of you. And there's so much to do before Sunday night. What first? In camper van circles it is customary to slide open the door, step outside in whatever you are wearing, yawn, say good morning to any other campers nearby and perhaps stretch a bit. It's not often you step straight out of bed and into the fresh air, so take a few deep breaths and say hello to a brand new, fun-filled day.

Next it's time to start thinking about breakfast. At the very least you will prepare the first brew of the day.

Assuming you've come prepared, all that remains is to decide what to have for your first breakfast in the wild. Did you bring some bake-to-take granola? Or did you pick up any free-range eggs at a roadside stall? If you didn't, you may well have to do the decent thing and leave everyone else to have a lie-in while you pull on your wellies and clomp off to the farm shop.

THE SEAGULL ALARM CLOCK

If you've been on the road the day before, you'll need a sure-fire way of waking up in time for the dawn surf. I don't suppose you brought an alarm clock, did you? No bother. Use this trick I learnt from the salty sea dogs of the North West Surf Club.

All you have to do is make a few handfuls of breadcrumbs. Creep out of your van once everyone else has gone to bed. Chuck the breadcrumbs on top of your van – or your mate's van. Go to bed knowing full well that, come the morning, the gulls are going to be all over the van as they noisily descend for a free breakfast. A tin roof will amplify the sound enormously. It never fails to work and can also be used to annoy neighbours who have kept you awake until the wee hours.

DAWN PATROL

My favourite way to start the day is by getting some proper exercise. For me, there's nothing more exhilarating than going surfing at first light. It's a little scary but nonetheless thrilling to paddle out in semi-darkness with nothing but the sound of the crashing surf to guide you. To see the sun rise over the dunes as you wait for waves, that's special.

If you are not a surfer then you can still enjoy the Dawn Patrol. Running, walking the dog, whatever, it still counts. It is amazing to be up before the rest of the world, doing something that makes you feel good. What better start to the day?

All surfers know that the first surf of the day is the best. Often the wind is lighter, there aren't many people about and the vibe in the water is much mellower. It's a nice feeling to know you've had the best of it when everyone else turns up and spoils the view.

Dawn Patrol BREAKFAST

Sometimes it's good to have a fry-up, granted. But when I am pottering about in Pootle I live partly under the misguided illusion that I am living a healthy life. So I like to eat well.

The Dawn Patrol Breakfast is a true breakfast of champions. It is a great reward for doing something that makes you feel good. If you've risen to the sound of bird-song and sweated a little in the misty, quiet hours then you deserve a tasty treat. It is as much about the experience as the food itself.

FOR 1

ONE VERY FINE VIEW, PREFERABLY OVERLOOKING EXCELLENT SURF (A FIELD WILL DO)

A DASH OF EARLY-MORNING SMUGNESS

GREEK YOGHURT

A BANANA (TO REPLACE YOUR SPENT ENERGY FROM YOUR DAWN PATROL ACTIVITY)

A HANDFUL OF CHOPPED NUTS (FOR PROTEIN)

CHOPPED DATES

A DRIZZLING OF CLEAR HONEY (WHY NOT? LIVE A LITTLE)

Prepare yourself by having a really good surf (or run or whatever). Find a vantage point. Scoop out a couple of big dollops of Greek yoghurt into the biggest bowl you can find. Add the banana (sliced), chuck in the nuts and dates. Drizzle the honey over the top. Eat. And while you're doing it, savour the view, enjoy the taste and relish the experience. See? I told you.

Lastly, go back to bed. It's far too early. Champion!

Once you've had your lie-in, it's time to get the rest of the troop up. One up, all up is what I say. Put the kettle on again and have a quick tidy up before flinging yourself into breakfast proper and getting another brew on. Whilst everyone heads off for their morning ablutions you'll be able to pack up the beds, tidy away your pyjamas, set up the table and get ready for a fabulous sunny-side-up breakfast in the great outdoors.

5-minute BANANA, HONEY and ORANGE smoothie

Bananas are great, yoghurt is great, honey is great, freshly squeezed orange juice is great. And that is why this is great. It's surprisingly filling too. Breakfast in a glass.

FOR 1 BIG GLASSFUL

1 BANANA
6 TBSP CHILLED NATURAL YOGHURT
1 TBSP OR SO RUNNY HONEY
FRESHLY SQUEEZED ORANGE JUICE

Peel, chop and mash the banana in a bowl. Stir in the yoghurt, about 1 tablespoon of honey and enough orange juice to give the smoothie the consistency you like. Taste and add more honey if needed. Drink chilled.

5-minute RASPBERRY, LIME and APPLE smoothie

Genius! It takes five minutes and contains raspberries and limes. Another breakfast favourite that's full of goodness. For a vitamin C hit, this is the one to go for.

FOR 2

2 GENEROUS HANDFULS (ABOUT 150G) RASPBERRIES
6 TBSP CHILLED NATURAL YOGHURT
1-2 TBSP RUNNY HONEY
JUICE OF $^1/_2$ LIME
CHILLED APPLE JUICE

Mash the raspberries in a bowl. Stir in the yoghurt, 1-2 tablespoons of honey, the lime juice and enough apple juice to give the smoothie the consistency you like. Taste and add more honey if needed. Drink chilled.

Exploding EGG Banjo

The exact origins of the Exploding Egg Banjo are unknown to me. For years I had thought it was just another name for a sandwich. A colloquialism. At the very most it could have been a speciality of the boys from the Leasowe Bay Surf Club. A peculiarity if you like, from a group of hooligans of the highest order. But no! When I started delving, and by that I mean Googling, I discovered that the Egg Banjo (or Exploding Egg Banjo) is not a sarnie or a butty or a sub or a Reg Varney, and it was not invented by Pete Windsor of the Wirral.

The ironic thing is that, like a fool who isn't in on the joke, I had been enjoying Exploding Egg Banjos for many, many years without understanding quite what I was doing. I was doing it right, it's just that I never quite made the connection. Doh! Try one yourself and you'll get it soon enough. The exploding bit is easy. It's the banjo part that promises – and delivers – that very brilliant eureka moment. Here's how to make your very own.

FOR 1

1 FRESH, FREE-RANGE EGG
1 SOFT BUTTERED WHITE ROLL
BROWN SAUCE
YOUR VERY BEST SHIRT

Fry the egg in oil until the white is cooked but the yolk is still runny. Place the egg in the buttered roll. Pour on a healthy dollop of brown sauce.

Now take a big bite of the sandwich. Don't be shy. The egg will explode and drip down your shirt in a big brown and yellow mess. Inevitably, you will hold the sandwich in one hand away from your body and brush the egg from your shirt with the other. Take a look at your body position. You are now eating an Exploding Egg sandwich. And playing an air banjo.

Breakfast FRITTATA

This is another way to go to work on an egg. The frittata is an Italian-style omelette that's great for camping because it's easy, quick to make and very fantastico. And kids love it.

Leave out the bacon and add a handful of chopped goat's cheese or halved cherry tomatoes for a delicious veggie version. You could also try using chopped spring onions for an extra little something.

FOR 2 OR 4, DEPENDING ON HOW HUNGRY YOU ARE

OIL

1 LARGE PEPPER, DESEEDED AND CHOPPED INTO BITE-SIZED CHUNKS

3 RASHERS BACON, CHOPPED

6 LARGE EGGS

2 ROUNDED TBSP SNIPPED CHIVES

2 ROUNDED TBSP GRATED PARMESAN

Heat a tablespoon of oil in a medium-sized frying pan and cook the pepper chunks for 5 minutes, or until softened. Next, stir in the bacon and cook with the pepper for a further 5 minutes, giving it a stir now and then. Meanwhile, crack the eggs into a bowl or jug and lightly beat them with the chives, Parmesan, a little salt and some freshly ground black pepper.

Once the pepper chunks are soft, pour in the egg mixture and leave to cook over a low-medium heat for 5-7 minutes, or until the bottom is golden and the top is set. Preheat the grill while the frittata is cooking. Next, put the pan under the grill and cook the frittata for a further 5-7 minutes, or until the top is golden brown. Cut into four wedges to eat.

THE EARLY BIRD CATCHES THE WORM

Now that you've had breakfast and have made yourself at home you might want to head off for a little exploration. What's the plan? You could do a lot worse than checking out some of the local inhabitants. Take out your wildlife guide, pack up a Thermos of tea and a couple of slices of tea bread, and go see some nature!

OUT AND ABOUT
THE RIGHT TO ROAM

The introduction of The Countryside and Rights of Way Act 2000 was a time to celebrate for ramblers and walkers who had been campaigning for the 'right to roam' for many years. But it still doesn't mean that you can go where you like. The so-called 'right to roam' gives rights of access – on foot – to mapped areas of "open country" in England. This is currently mountain, moor, heathland, downland and registered common land. So, if you're not absolutely sure that the land you are on is considered to be "open country", stick to footpaths.

In Scotland everyone has the right to be on most land, providing they act responsibly, though of course there are always exceptions. And there are rules to obey and guidelines to follow, but that's not so bad, is it?

The Countryside Code
Be safe, plan ahead and follow any signs
Leave gates and property as you find them
Protect plants and animals and take your litter home
Keep dogs under close control
Consider other people

TRESPASS LAW

Trespass is the act of going on to land which is not a right of way, common land or open access land without permission. It is a civil offence to trespass and you can therefore be taken to court for it, but this is pretty unlikely to happen unless you do it repeatedly. More likely than not, if you trespass, intentionally or unintentionally, then the land owner will ask you to leave. I'd say, apologise and move on.

THE WEATHER

"Rain rain go away, come again another day."

One of the best things about camper van living is that the weather, unless it's really bad for days on end, can't affect you as much as it might if you were living under canvas. Happily, your van is your own little home and unless you're experiencing the very worst extremes of weather you're going to be warm, dry, well fed and comfortable.

In a primal way, your van is your cave. So whilst all the other campers are rushing around pegging out, searching for the pac a macs and singing cheery songs to keep them from the depths of camping despair, you're going to be cuddling up in your own watertight space with a cup of tea and a slice of delicious flapjack. In time the shower will pass and you'll emerge from your cosy camping cocoon, ready to carry on with your day.

During the hottest heatwave your camper van will give you shade and during the worst winter storms the stove (or the central heating if you've got it installed) will keep you warm. You're more likely to suffer from cabin fever than you are to drown or freeze to death. Boredom, the real killer, will get you before anything else. But not if you've remembered to pack your top locker with plenty of exciting games and books! After that you're on your own.

"I spy with my little eye, something beginning with R"
"Rain?"
"Yup. Your turn."
And so on.

WEATHER FORECASTING THE COUNTRY WAY

Is it true that cows will sit down if it's going to rain? If you lived in a field, would you prefer to sit down while it was still dry or after it had started raining? I know what I'd prefer.

Before the days of internet forecasting, iPhones and telly, people used to look to nature for their forecasts. It was important – and it's something many of us have lost the ability to do. All we have left are a few phrases and sayings.

But do they work? Camper van living is all about going outside, braving the weather and living a little more in harmony with nature, so why not see whether they work for you.

When the dew is on the grass, rain will never come to pass
When grass is dry at morning light, look for rain before the night
This one's all about the air temperature cooling rapidly and depositing moisture. If it's cold at night it usually means the sky is cloudless, which means no rain. Maybe.

Red sky at night, shepherds' delight
Red sky in the morning, shepherds' warning
Who hasn't heard this one? It's all to do with atmospheric pressure, dust particles, the spectrum and rising air. Don't go there. Just believe.

Cats leap about and chase their tails to warn of thunderstorms and gales
Cats, like many animals, are sensitive to atmospheric pressure. Their behaviour may well be linked to the atmosphere – a bit like we feel a little 'electric' before a big thunderstorm. Don't you? I do.

Seagull, seagull, stay on the sand. It's never fair weather if you're over land
Seagulls are sea birds and feed at sea – usually. But if the weather is bad you can't blame them for not wanting to risk it. The sea can be a nasty place. Better to steal chips from tourists on the seafront instead.

Birds fly high in a summer sky

During periods of high pressure birds fly higher because conditions are stiller. If you were a bird would you want to fly against strong winds in bad weather? Me neither. But is it true? Keep your eyes peeled and find out.

Mackerel sky and mares' tails make tall ships carry small sails

Have you ever heard of a mackerel sky? It's when cirrocumulus clouds form, which are often associated with rain showers. Having said that, a drop of fishy rain could well save you from another disappointing fishing trip. If there's a mackerel sky, put out a bucket. Just in case.

Cows all lying down together are a sign of rain

As I said before, would you lie in the wet patch? No. Exactly.

WATCHING THE WILDLIFE

My very learned friend Dave works for the RSPB. He's mad about the outdoors so I asked him to put together a list of brilliant places to see wildlife in the UK and Ireland. Wherever you are there's always something very special to see.

NOTES ON WHALE AND DOLPHIN WATCHING

The best time to see whales or dolphins is in the summer and early autumn. With the sun behind you as you look out to sea you'll enjoy better visibility. On western-facing coasts this will generally be in the morning. Get a good position on a clifftop and take a pair of binoculars.

Of course whales and dolphins spend a fair amount of time under water, and this makes them quite hard to spot. So don't expect too much. However, the more you look, the more you see. Keep your eyes peeled!

THE NEW FOREST

All of Britain's reptile species can be found here including adders, grass snakes, the very rare smooth snake and the even rarer sand lizard (Britain's rarest reptile). These can be a bit shy. It is an offence to disturb the smooth snake or the sand lizard, so you may be best going to the New Forest Reptile Centre near Lyndhurst to get a proper look.

EAST ANGLIA

The East Anglian coast still has a real feel of wilderness about it. It's famous among birdwatchers. Everyone can get something out of coming here, with ringed plover, redshank and lapwing spotted in the summer and brent geese in the winter. It is one of the few places left where you might hear the boom of the bittern.

It's fun to take a trip to see the seals beyond Blakeney Point. Check online for details. Further south, the National Nature Reserve at Walberswick is home to hundreds of birds, insects, plants and mammals, including five species of deer.

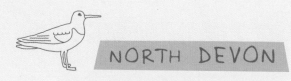

NORTH DEVON

The Biosphere Reserve, a World Heritage Site designated by the United Nations for its unique landscapes and biodiversity, is centred around the dune system at Braunton Burrows. It extends to most of the North Devon coast and much of the Taw and Torridge Estuary. Wildlife to be seen here includes seabirds, wading birds, otters, dormice, rare lichens and butterflies, as well as seals and dolphins off Lundy Island. The island itself is perhaps best known for Devon's only breeding colony of puffins.

CORNWALL

In the summer the world's second-biggest fish, the basking shark, visits the plankton-rich waters off Cornwall and Devon. They can grow up to 11 metres in length. Another marine giant, the ocean sunfish, the heaviest bony fish in the world, also visits the Cornish coast in the summer months to feed on jellyfish. You stand a good chance of seeing them both from Porthgwarra near Land's End, but if you are lucky you might see them from any headland in West Cornwall. These are also great places to see common and bottle-nosed dolphins, grey seals and seabirds aplenty.

NORTHUMBERLAND

With beautiful beaches, fabulous ruined castles and amazing wildlife, Northumberland is a quiet corner of England where you can see spectacular sights without the crowds. Seabirds abound. A trip to the Farne Islands in the spring or early summer can yield sightings of puffins, eider ducks, terns and shags at close quarters.

Northumberland is also one of the few places in the UK where you might still see red squirrels; head to Wallington, owned by the National Trust. And for old castles you can't beat Dunstanburgh with its stunning clifftop setting.

PEMBROKESHIRE, SOUTH WALES

St Davids is situated in a very good area for wildlife. Ramsey Island, which lies offshore to the west, is home to seabirds such as puffins and manx shearwaters, as well as to the chough, a rare member of the crow family with red legs and beak.

Ramsey Sound, the stretch of water between the island and the mainland, is a great place to look for harbour porpoises, whether from the island, the mainland or from the boat in between the two. Look out for puffins on Skomer Island, off the Marloes peninsula, while Strumble Head, to the north of St Davids, is a good place to look for dolphins, whales and seabirds. In the heathland gorse, unique to northern Europe, you might find adders, spot the insect world's fastest runner, the tiger beetle, or see rare fritillary butterflies.

LLYN PENINSULA AND HARLECH BAY, NORTH WALES

Bottle-nosed dolphins can be seen from springtime through to the summer off Abersoch. A good place to look from is Cilan Head, which is also home to the minotaur beetle (a large black beetle that looks like a mini triceratops), the green tiger beetle and more choughs. The bay at Porth Ceiriad is also a regular spot for dolphins. In summer you might see a leatherback turtle in Harlech Bay. They follow their favourite dinner, jellyfish, here.

MULL, NORTH WEST SCOTLAND

The waters around Mull are home to bottle-nosed dolphins, minke whales and harbour porpoises. Risso's dolphins, killer whales, common dolphins and Atlantic white-sided dolphins are also regular visitors. It is probably worth a look from any headland and in the larger sea lochs, but good spots include Tobermory lighthouse for harbour porpoises and Iona Sound for bottle-nosed dolphins. You're also likely to see harbour porpoises from the Oban-Mull ferry. The Hebridean Whale and

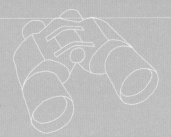

Dolphin Trust has a marine discovery centre in Tobermory,
from where you can also take a trip in a whale-watching boat.

   Mull is rich in wildlife. You might also spot common or grey
seals, sea otters, red deer, or even golden eagles and sea eagles.

THE MINCHES, NORTH WEST SCOTLAND

The Minch and the Little Minch are the straits that separate the Outer Hebrides from
Skye and mainland Scotland. The Straits are a very good place to see dolphins,
porpoises, basking sharks and minke whales during the summer. They are often
spotted from the Caledonian MacBrayne ferries which cross to the Outer Hebrides.

SOUTH WEST IRELAND

The whale-watching capital of northern Europe! You would be hard pushed to visit
South West Ireland and not see dolphins at the very least. It is the best place Dave
knows for seeing minke whales. It is also home to the second largest animal on
Earth, the fin whale. Second in size only to the blue whale, which has also been seen
here, fin whales are regular visitors. With a fair dollop of luck they can be seen from
land, but a boat trip from West Cork is probably a better bet. November is one of
the best months. For regular spotting you won't need your sea legs: minke whales,
bottle-nosed dolphins and harbour porpoises can all be seen from land. Basking
sharks, ocean sunfish, grey and common seals, seabirds and choughs can all be seen
in this area too (and the Guinness really is better in Ireland).

ELEVENSES

Elevenses is a special time of the day. Funnily enough, it happens at around eleven o'clock in the morning, a time that's a respectful enough distance between breakfast and lunch. If you're inclined to be a very early or late riser, elevenses can be a moveable feast, but accepted wisdom agrees that it should never be after 12. That would be rude.

Many people consider elevenses to be a bit old hat these days. And it probably is. But who says that new is always better? I think elevenses should be observed simply because it's a time for a cuppa and a little perk-me-up before lunch. It is a reward for the early risers and shouldn't be confused with brunch, which is for people who've got up so late that they've missed breakfast. Elevenses is the time to down tools and take stock of the morning's work. Nothing serious happens food-wise, just something sweet to take the edge off the pre-lunch hunger. A catch-up and a mini-break before the sun is too high in the sky.

THE PERFECT CUPPA

★ Always use boiling water. Let the kettle whistle for while.
★ Warm the pot or mugs with a little hot water.
★ Take the pot or the mugs to the kettle and pour the water on to the bags. Don't add the bags to water.
★ Let the tea steep for a minute or so. Do not stir.
★ Put your tea bags in the compost (on site or back at home), not the bin.
★ Milk should be added to the tea, never the other way round.
★ Don't slurp. It's rude.

Sarah likes
medium
strength

Martin likes
strong
but milky

Jo likes
builder's brew

FRUIT and NUT crispies

MAKES 15

12 SQUARES (ABOUT 75G) MILK CHOCOLATE

3 TBSP (ABOUT 50G) BUTTER

3 TBSP GOLDEN SYRUP

3 GENEROUS TBSP RAISINS

3 MUGFULS (ABOUT 75G) RICE KRISPIES

2 TBSP CHOPPED PECANS (OR OTHER NUTS)

In a pan, slowly melt half the chocolate with the butter and syrup. Give it a stir from time to time. Tip in the raisins and Rice Krispies, take off the heat, mix and leave to cool for 15 minutes.

Chop the rest of the chocolate into small pieces. Stir the pecans and the chopped chocolate into the Rice Krispies mix and spoon into 15 paper cases (or into round blobs on a baking tray). Chill for 30 minutes before devouring.

ROCKY ROAD on the ROAD

Elevenses isn't a time for watching your figure. It's a celebration of your morning's work. And if you've been working hard putting up awnings, entertaining kids or just hanging out at base camp you deserve a really sweet treat. I loved making this and could hardly keep my hands out of the cookie jar afterwards. I am pretty sure you won't be able to either. Be warned – it is very moreish.

MAKES 16 SQUARES

150G BUTTER

4 TBSP GOLDEN SYRUP OR RUNNY HONEY

400G MILK CHOCOLATE, BROKEN INTO SQUARES

10 PINK AND WHITE MARSHMALLOWS (ABOUT 100G)

12 DIGESTIVE OR OTHER SWEETMEAL BISCUITS (ABOUT 150G)

20 GLACE CHERRIES (ABOUT 100G)

4 TBSP SULTANAS

In a pan over a low heat, gently melt the butter with the golden syrup or honey and the chocolate. Cool the mixture while you chop the rest of the ingredients.

Chop the marshmallows and biscuits and quarter the cherries. Stir these and the sultanas into the chocolate mixture and mix together. Tip the mixture into a lightly buttered 20cm, shallow-sided square cake tin (or similar-sized dish – we used a handy Tupperware box). Cool and chill to set, 2-3 hours should do it. Cut into chunky squares – or bars if you prefer.

VW CAMPER VAN CULTURE

There's an awful lot more to camper van culture than a little bit of happy-go-lucky waving across the central reservation and mutual back-slapping. People really do love their VW campers and aren't afraid to show it or discuss it at great length. Visit a VW show and you'll meet people who live and breathe camper vans. You'll always meet someone who knows an awful lot more about them than you do. In my experience people are very friendly and more than happy to pass on their knowledge to others who are willing to lap it up. Take a look at the show 'n' shine to see just how much love and attention the hardcore enthusiasts lavish on their vehicles. It really is astounding.

If you've got a van, are thinking about buying one, have rented one for the weekend or have borrowed one for a trip away, you could do worse than taking a day out to visit a VW show (for suggestions, see the list on page 273). You will see some truly remarkable vehicles. Everything from tatty, 'rat look' splitties to super-shiny, money-no-object restorations will be on show, ready for you to gawp at. In fact, gawping is what you'll end up doing. You'll never see so many beautiful objects of desire in one place.

Fast behind the shows come VW fan sites, forums, parts suppliers, magazines and specialist retailers. They are great places to find a van or a few rare spares and advice. You can even get someone to run up a brand new pair of curtains for you.

From personal experience I can tell you that it's worth hooking into this kind of thing. When I bought Pootle I joined the 80-90 Club, a really friendly T25 club with a lively forum. I needed some spare shelves for my fridge so posted a link. Three days later a set turned up in the post. How about that for service?

TAKE A VISIT TO AN ODD GOING ON

There's nowt so queer as folk. It's true. They do all sorts of bonkers things with their spare time. All over the place people are finding good reasons to get together and re-enact traditions, make up their own, take part in impossible sports, poke fun at authority or just have a jolly good laugh. It's worth a look.

STRAW BEAR FESTIVAL, Whittlesea, Cambridgeshire,
January, first Monday after Twelfth Night
A tradition dating back to the 1800s that sees a member of the community wrapped in straw and paraded round town on a leash. The 'bear' is forced to dance in exchange for money and beer.

BRIGHTON BEACH SWIM, *Christmas Morning*
I'll go in the sea on Christmas Day for a surf but not without a wetsuit. This lot, like many others around the UK, do it in fancy dress. I'll bet there's a few with wetties underneath.

CHEESE ROLLING, Brookworth, Gloucestershire, *Spring Bank Holiday Monday*
All you have to do is chase a cheese down a hill. What could be so hard about that? But have you seen the hill? Injuries are common.

TAR BARREL RACING, Ottery St. Mary, Devon, *November 5th*
"Here mate, take this flaming barrel of tar and run as fast as you can with it." "OK." Really? Health and Safety would hate it but it's good fun to watch and finishes with an almighty bonfire.

SHROVETIDE FOOTBALL, Ashbourne, Derbyshire, *Shrove Tuesday and Ash Wednesday*
The largest football match in the world, with hundreds of players on each team. The playing field is three miles long and two miles wide, with the village in the middle. Bonkers.

COTSWOLD OLIMPICKS, Dover's Hill, Gloucestershire,
May, Friday after Spring Bank Holiday
How about entering a shin kicking contest? Why not? Sounds like fun. Less hardy souls go for the morris dancing, obstacle races and tug-of-war.

NUTTERS DANCE, Bacup, Lancashire, *Easter Saturday*
There is a fascinating history to the Britannia Coco-Nut Dancers, some of which may or may not be true. Who knows the true origins? Miners from Cornwall or Pagan ritual? This is the ultimate folk dance, performed by nutters in funny costumes.

HAXEY HOOD GAME, Haxey, North Lincolnshire, *Twelfth Day of Christmas*
People in crazy costumes fight over a symbolic hood. Sounds simple but there's a lot more to it than that. Pomp and ceremony abound in this 650-year-old game where a scrum of a few hundred people try to get to the pub. Sounds like a good Friday night out. Go see for yourself.

BOG SNORKELLING CHAMPIONSHIPS, Waen Rhydd peat bog, Llanwrtyd Wells, *August Bank Holiday*
I dunno. Snorkelling in a bog? What were they thinking of? So successful they now do a bog snorkelling triathlon and other such nonsense. Don't miss it.

THE ANCIENT FIREBALLS CEREMONY, High Street, Stonehaven, *New Year's Eve*
Great balls of fire. Literally. Sixty locals swinging balls of fire make this one torchlight parade with a difference.

TEDFEST, Inis Mór, off the coast of County Galway, *last weekend in February*
An annual event celebrating the life of Father Ted. Feck! Lovely girls, fags and drenk assured. Book me in!!!!

SATURDAY LUNCH

Back to nature

Let's start thinking about lunch. When we're out in the wild we are surrounded by food. The trouble is that we've forgotten just how much out there can be eaten. As a result, we find it hard to go out into the fields or along the seashore and find a little food for ourselves.

LET'S GO WILD
(Or why foraging is better than shopping)

Something as simple as a bowl of freshly picked blackberries can be really satisfying. Much as the miser in me thinks it's because it's free, it's deeper than that. It's the hunter-gatherer instinct. It's making a point of not going to the supermarket. It's doing things the hard way. It's making an adventure out of eating. For many of us, who have everything laid out in front of us at the supermarket, it is a little taste of the freshest produce we'll ever get our hands on. And that's got to be worth trying.

So if you're ready, let's go wild.

SOME BASIC PRINCIPLES OF FORAGING

Whether you do your foraging in the countryside or by the seashore there are some very important rules and guidelines to follow.

Invest in a good field guide. I keep a pocket-sized version of Richard Mabey's amazing *Food for Free* in the van. It is really useful and can help to confirm that what I am picking is what I think it is. There are lots of other guide books with clear photographs and detailed information available, so it's worth finding one that you like.

Read a little, learn a little and you'll be alright. Better still, go out with a professional forager for the day and learn from them – some run courses. You might want to plan your camper van weekend round one of those.

Remember that taking fungi, fruit and foliage from the countryside is ok if you are taking for non-commercial use and have the permission of the land owner. That makes foraging in open access land perfectly acceptable as long as you don't intend to go into business.

★ Take only what you need and no more.
★ Be absolutely positive in your identification before taking anything.
★ Eat what you know.
★ Don't remove all stocks from one place. Give them a chance to regrow.
★ Do not forage for endangered species or pick rare plants. Know which ones are which.
★ When picking shellfish or crustaceans make sure you only take those above the legally permitted minimum size.
★ If you are taking shrimps, prawns or lobsters, put back any pregnant females, irrespective of size.
★ Don't trespass. Get the permission of the landowner.
★ Never pick from the verges of busy roads or where there is industry or pollution.
★ Do your best not to harm or injure anything else when you are looking for your catch, particularly in rock pools.

LEARNING TO LOVE THE COAST
(Or how not to get rescued)

Whatever you intend to do at the coast – foraging, beachcombing, taking part in a beach clean, surfing or just having a lazy day out – it's vital to understand just a little about it. If you don't, you can unwittingly get into all sorts of trouble. While it might sound like fun to get a lift home in a helicopter or on a lifeboat, it really isn't. And it can cost a lot more than cold hard cash.

GETTING TO KNOW HOW TIDES WORK

Some people are surprised that the tides are different every day. They visit one week and find the tide in and then come back a week later to find the sea gone. No, really. Of course we wouldn't think such nonsense! But would we?

On foraging adventures it's easy to forget where you are and what time the tides are. You can approximate the height of the next high tide by looking at the top of the beach. If there is a line of seaweed along it, then the next high tide will come up as far as the line of seaweed that's nearest to the sea (give or take a few metres).

High and low tide times change by about an hour every day – and with every location – so it's always a good idea to get a copy of a local tide table.

Tides are governed by the phases of the moon, so like the moon, tides go in cycles. During full and new moons – actually just after – we experience spring tides. This is when the tidal range is greatest and the sea comes in further up the beach and goes out further than at any other time. Neap tides – during the first and third quarter in moon terms – are those that have the smallest tidal range. These changes in tidal ranges mean that you could find yourself walking along a beach at high tide one week and the next week, at high tide, the beach could be completely covered with water. Assuming you are safe from the tide 'because that's where it comes up to' could easily lead you to think you won't get cut off. But if you've guessed incorrectly while exploring some far-flung cove, that's exactly what can happen.

Spring tides come in and go out quicker than at any other time – because there is further to travel and the same amount of time to do it in. In some places, where the beaches are very flat, the tide can really rush in. Whether or not the tide could 'overtake a galloping horse' (as the stories go) in these places is not for me to say as I have never tested it out (no horse). But places like the Severn Estuary, where lots of water rushes up a narrowing river mouth, have tides that form river waves (or bores) that are so powerful they can even be surfed.

DON'T BE AFRAID TO ASK

If you're planning on heading off to do some foraging, or even for a walk along the coast, the best people to talk to are the locals. The saltier the better. As well as giving advice on where to find what (a pint might be a small price to pay) they will be able to let you know what to watch out for along the way. They might even point you in the direction of a few hidden gems. Or not, depending on how many pints you bought them.

Time and Tide wait for no man

For me, picking mussels is one of the classic foraging adventures. They are fun to find, free to pick, easy to cook, hard to spoil and create hardly any washing-up. They are even good for your conscience because they are on the Marine Conservation Society's green light list of sustainable seafood. An added bonus is that they are absolutely delicious.

Have you ever heard the old wives' tale that you should only ever eat mussels when there is an 'R' in the month? The reason for this is that the summer months (May to August) are spawning time for a lot of seafood. To help our little bivalve friends in their battle for long-term survival we have to allow them their fun too. Leave them alone and you'll be rewarded come the autumn.

Once you have found where the mussels live, remember the foraging rules and take only what you need. The best time to pick them is on a low spring tide. The biggest will be found towards low water. If you can, pick those that are clean and free from seaweed and barnacles. It'll save time later.

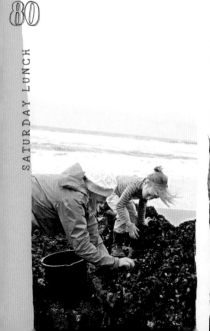

CLEANING AND PREPARING

Preparation is key so it's worth taking the time. Each mussel has a beard – a bunch of hairy fibres that it uses to cling to the rock. You'll need to pull these off. A little twist and a pull should do it. Discard any mussels that are broken. Put the mussels in clean fresh water with a little dash of vinegar. This will help to clean them and encourage them to spit out their grit.

Rinse them a couple of times and clean off any barnacles or seaweed. If any are floating, or are open, discard them.

COOKING MUSSELS

Steaming is the basic method for cooking mussels. Put a little liquid in the bottom of a pan on a high heat, chuck in the mussels, cover and steam until they begin to open (usually only a few minutes). That's it really. You could even cook them over a beach fire if you wanted to. The variations are all about the juices and you won't need any other major ingredients. One thing to remember, though, is that you should only eat the ones that are open. Always discard those that are closed.

Don't throw your discarded mussel shells in the bin once you've eaten. Since you're at the beach, you can rinse them thoroughly and then put them back on the beach, below the high tide mark. In time they will become sand.

MOULES in coconut milk and CORIANDER

I absolutely adore coriander so I love to use loads of it, the fresher the better. This recipe for Thai-style moules more than satisfies my coriander cravings. It is simple and fresh with a little bit of the spicy stuff. Perfect for slurping. Hopefully you'll have garlic and a tin of coconut milk at the back of the van's cupboards somewhere so your daily shopping list is meagre. The main ingredient, of course, is free.

FOR 2

OLIVE OIL

SMALL KNOB OF BUTTER

1 RED CHILLI, FINELY CHOPPED, DESEEDED IF YOU LIKE THINGS MILD, OR A GOOD PINCH
   OF CRUSHED DRIED CHILLI (DON'T GO CRAZY – YOU DON'T WANT TO OVERPOWER IT!)

2 CLOVES GARLIC, FINELY CHOPPED

JUICE OF 1 LIME

KNOB OF FRESH ROOT GINGER, ABOUT 2CM, PEELED AND GRATED

2 SPRING ONIONS, CHOPPED

1 X 160ML TIN COCONUT MILK

6 DOUBLE HANDFULS (ABOUT 4KG) CLEANED AND PREPARED MUSSELS

LARGE HANDFUL CORIANDER

CRUSTY BREAD, TO SERVE

Pour a splash of oil into a large pan and add the butter, then heat together. Add the chilli, garlic, lime, ginger and spring onions. Fry for a couple of moments then pour in the coconut milk, bring to the boil and simmer for a few minutes. Tip in the mussels, bring the liquid back to the boil and cover. Steam the mussels for 3-4 minutes, giving the pan a shake occasionally.

Take the lid off and discard any mussels that have refused to open during cooking, then add the coriander. Stir and serve the mussels steaming hot in bowls with a chunk of crusty white bread, while overlooking your favourite mussel-picking haunt.

Top it off with a very cold beer, preferably Singha to keep the Thai vibe going, and perhaps a bit of an afternoon snooze in a deckchair.

Camper van MOULES

This is a super-easy way to cook mussels and can be done on one ring. It's my favourite too because it's really salty and fresh – a real taste of the sea – with a tangy burst of fresh celery to spice it up a bit. You can use the base of a steamer to cook in or any big pan with a lid will do. Good with fat doorsteps of fresh crusty bread and butter and a cool glass of white wine.

FOR 4

1 LARGE ONION
2 CLOVES GARLIC
OLIVE OIL
KNOB OF BUTTER
2 OR 3 CELERY STICKS, CHOPPED
HANDFUL CHOPPED PARSLEY
LARGE GLASS OF WHITE WINE
6 DOUBLE HANDFULS (ABOUT 4KG) CLEANED AND PREPARED MUSSELS
CRUSTY BREAD, TO SERVE

Peel and chop the onion and peel and slice the garlic. Heat a splash of oil and the butter in a large frying pan, then add the onion, garlic and celery. Fry over a medium heat for 8-10 minutes or until the onions soften. Add a sprinkle of ground black pepper and most of the parsley. Pour in the wine and tip in the mussels. Bring everything up to simmering point, then cover and cook the mussels for 3-4 minutes or until their shells open (discard any that don't), giving the pot an occasional shake as the mussels cook.

Bingo! That's it. Serve in bowls, scattered with the remaining parsley. Don't even bother with spoons and forks – you can use an empty shell like tweezers to pick out the mussels. And when it comes to the fresh, salty juice, just soak it up with plenty of bread.

SHRIMPING AND PRAWNING

Seaside foraging, especially on sunny summer days, is an absolute delight. Give me a hot sun high in a summer sky, a whisper of a breeze to cool the air and a rockpool to rummage in and you'll find me at my happiest, searching for a treat among the seaweed. Shrimping and prawning is fantastic fun. If you're lucky enough to catch some you'll feel a wave of excitement every time you see one flip about in your net. You can catch shrimps and prawns all around the coast if you know where to look. It's not even that difficult. All you need is the right equipment, a bit of patience and someone to share your catch with.

You can catch brown shrimp on sandy and silty estuarine beaches with a push net. These are traditional wooden nets with a handle and a wooden T-bar at the end. A thick wire D-shaped hoop holds a long net. To use them you simply hold the handle and push the T-bar along the bottom near the shore. The movement of the bar disturbs the shrimps from their semi-covered hiding places (they only come out at night). As they panic at your rude interruption you scoop them up in your net. It's an age-old technique that works a treat – if you do it where the shrimpies live. If you don't you'll just get wet and cold.

When it comes to exciting rockpooling adventures, going prawning is second only to poking about for lobster. You never know what else might turn up in your net. We've had cuttlefish, crabs, tiny turbots, heaps of blennies, loads of tiddlers and a few sand eels. Every new find brings squeals of delight as the lucky prawner peers into their net to see what's been caught. It's an adventure and an education as well as a shopping trip with a difference. As another cry of "Oh yes, look at the size of that one!" drifts across the rocks, everyone stops to admire the latest whopper in the bucket.

To catch your quota of prawns you need a big low tide to get at all the choicest rock pools. You'll also need a good dip net. This is like a sturdier version of the classic rockpooling net. The extra strength allows you to dip it in rockpools and 'tickle' the seaweed without bending or breaking. 'Cupping' the seaweed bunches with your net and shaking them gently will disturb any prawns living or hiding there. As you lift the net out of the water you should bring any prawns with you.

COOKING YOUR CATCH

Why wait until you get back to the van when you can cook your catch right there on the sand? Prawns don't need much cooking, so a small burner and a mess tin or a small saucepan will do it. Boil up some water (sea water is OK) and chuck the prawns in whole. In just a couple of minutes they'll turn beautifully pink and ready for eating. Drain them and they are ready to serve. You can pull their heads off and peel them or eat them whole, it's up to you. We love them with a simple and easy-to-make home-made dip. They don't need much else.

Of course if you are a little too squeamish for eating things that are just out of the sea, nip in to the fishmonger's on the way to the beach. North Atlantic prawns are the ones to go for. Take a jar of dipping mayo with you and you'll still be able to enjoy all the excitement of prawning (after you've eaten your shop-bought shellfish!) with the added pleasure of putting them back afterwards.

Tiger prawns are farmed using questionable practices so, while they look delicious, it is best to avoid them. The Marine Conservation Society has them on their 'fish to avoid' list.

THE LOBSTER HUNT

Of all the foraging prizes (apart from truffles, perhaps) lobster is the daddy of them all. Finding and catching a lobster is one of the most exciting foraging adventures you could have. A lot of the lobster that finds its way on to the fishmonger's ice in the UK is caught in pots from boats, but they can be discovered under rocks and in rocky caves at very low tides on some beaches. All you have to do is poke about in a few holes with a lobster gaff and see what comes up. Gaffs are basically sticks with hooks on the end. You can make one with a piece of bamboo and a coat hanger. Good luck!

Crawfish, which are also known as spiny lobster, are now very rare. So if you find one, do not take it, whatever its size.

The minimum legal take size for European Lobster is 9cm measured in a straight line from the back of the eye socket to the end of the body not including the tail.

In many places it is illegal to take female lobsters with eggs, irrespective of the size. If you find a berried female (a lobster with eggs underneath), put her back straight away.

If you find a lobster with a V-shaped notch cut into the tail, put it back. These are from breeding programmes.

If you do catch a lobster that isn't carrying eggs, hasn't been notched and is of legal size, stop right there. One is enough.

RAZOR CLAMS

Razor clams are delicious but hard to catch. They bury themselves deep in the sand and it takes a little coaxing to get them out. The trick is to fool them into thinking the sea has returned (you go looking for them on very low spring tides) with a little pile of salt.

Head out at low tide and look out for their oval breathing holes or where they have buried themselves quickly in the sand. Pour a little salt into the hole and wait. If you are lucky they will pop up. All you have to do is grab them and gently prise them out of their burrows. Easier said than done. Enjoy.

LIMPETS

Until I first tried limpets at my local beach about ten years ago they had only ever been bashed off the rocks for crab bait. I had never considered them fit for human consumption. But they are.

Anyway, Gary the knee (not his real name), an expert camper van dweller, was the first person to persuade me to eat a limpet. The sun was going down, the surf was up, they were cooked over an open fire, I was curious. It was still a last resort though, and always will be. As usual take only what you need and take them from a wide area.

CLAMS AND COCKLES

These small bivalves live side by side in the sand and silt of river estuaries at the coast. They are equally delicious and can be used in similar dishes.

You can find clams and cockles all round the coast at low tide (especially spring tides). Check first before collecting, as some local authorities allow only licensed pickers to harvest. Watch out for incoming tides and take someone with you in case you get stuck in the mud.

To gather them you don't even need to take a rake (the traditional method of finding them) because you can search them out with your size nines as you walk over the mud flats – brilliant fun! If you like getting messy and feeling mud ooze and squelch between your toes then this is for you. Simply feel your way through the mud with your toes as you take each step. When you feel something hard, do a little digging with your hands. It could well be a cockle or a clam. Check it's above the minimum size (20mm), chuck it in a bucket and carry on.

88

LOBSTER salad

Fancy a lobster salad but can't find a lobster to go with it? Go to the nearest port and buy one from a fisherman or nip into the fishmonger's. After a day hunting for the elusive lobster you'll deserve a glass of chilled white wine to go with this decadent salad.

FOR 2
HALF A CUCUMBER
1 RED OR PINK GRAPEFRUIT
1 RIPE BUT FIRM AVOCADO
4 GENEROUS HANDFULS MIXED SALAD LEAVES (BABY LEAF SALAD IS IDEAL)
2 SMALL (OR 1 LARGE) COOKED LOBSTERS, MEAT REMOVED AND CHOPPED INTO
  BITE-SIZED PIECES

FOR THE DRESSING
1 TBSP THAI SWEET CHILLI SAUCE
JUICE OF 2 LIMES
2 TSP FINELY CHOPPED ROOT GINGER
1 TBSP OLIVE OIL

Halve the cucumber lengthways, then slice each half into half-moon shapes. Using a sharp knife, slice off either end of the grapefruit and stand it upright on a board, then slice the peel off, cutting downwards around the shape of the fruit. Slice the grapefruit into rounds and cut each round into quarters. Halve, peel and de-stone the avocado, slice it and then cut each slice in half. For the dressing, mix all the ingredients together.

In a large bowl, toss all the prepared salad ingredients together with the salad leaves, lobster meat and the dressing, adding a generous pinch of crushed sea salt. Pile into deep bowls or on to plates to eat.

A pint of PRAWNS and MAYO

Here are two fantastic – and very quick – dips to dunk your prawns in. With freshly-caught shrimps cooked right on the beach it makes for a feast of the highest order and proves once again that simple is best. Use the best-quality mayonnaise you can find as it'll make a big difference to the flavour.

Smoked PAPRIKA mayo

 8 TBSP MAYONNAISE
½ TSP SWEET SMOKED PAPRIKA

Mix together, adding a pinch of sea salt.

LIME and CHILLI mayo

If you are feeding kids, this one works just as well without the chilli – but obviously has less of a kick.

 8 TBSP MAYONNAISE
ZEST OF 2 LIMES
GENEROUS SQUEEZE OF LIME JUICE
GENEROUS PINCH CRUSHED DRIED CHILLIES

Mix together with a pinch of sea salt, taste and add a little more lime juice if needed.

GARLICKY razor clams

Straight from the beach, a quick rinse and into a hot pan and you have a feast for two fit for a king. A spoonful of the smoked paprika mayo on page 90 would be good too, swirled into the juices.

FOR 2

12 RAZOR CLAMS
OLIVE OIL
TUMBLER OF WHITE WINE
2 TBSP SOFT BUTTER
1 FAT CLOVE GARLIC, CRUSHED, OR 1 TBSP CHOPPED WILD GARLIC LEAVES
2-3 TBSP CHOPPED PARSLEY
CRUSTY BREAD, TO SERVE

Rinse the clams well in cold water. Tip them into a pan with a drizzle of olive oil and the wine. Bring the liquid to the boil, add a lid and simmer the clams for 3-4 minutes or until the shells have steamed open.

Remove the lid, add the butter and garlic or wild garlic leaves and scatter with the parsley. Put the lid back on, leave the pan over the heat for a minute or so, then give the pan a good shake so the flavours mingle.

Tip into bowls and tuck in with plenty of bread to dip into the juices – pull the long meaty part from each clam to eat them, discarding the dark bit at the end of each one as it is often tough.

Linguine with CLAMS, COCKLES, MUSSELS and watercress

If you have some to hand, add a couple of rashers of bacon, chopped, to the onion when you cook this recipe. And cook it overlooking the beach if you can.

FOR 4
500G CLAMS
500G COCKLES
500G MUSSELS, SCRUBBED AND BEARDS REMOVED
1 ONION, CHOPPED
OLIVE OIL
3 CLOVES GARLIC, FINELY CHOPPED
300G DRIED LINGUINE (OR SPAGHETTI)
SMALL TUMBLER OF FINO SHERRY, DRY WHITE WINE OR CIDER
3 TBSP CRÈME FRAICHE OR CREAM
2 GENEROUS HANDFULS CHOPPED WATERCRESS (OR ROCKET)

Rinse the shellfish under cold running water and discard any shells that don't close shut when given a sharp tap. Bring a pan of salted water to the boil for the pasta.

In another pan, gently cook the onion in 3 tablespoons of olive oil until soft, 10 minutes or so, then stir in the garlic and cook for a further few minutes. Cook the pasta according to the pack instructions.

Meanwhile, tip the shellfish into the pan with the onion, along with the sherry, and bring to simmering point. Cover with a lid and cook for 5-6 minutes, giving the pan a shake now and then until the shells have opened (discard any that refuse to).

Using a slotted spoon or similar, remove the shellfish to a bowl with the oniony bits (don't worry if there are a few left), reserving the liquid. When it's cooked, drain the linguine, return to its pan and toss over the heat with plenty of seasoning, the crème fraiche and the watercress.

Strain the liquid from the shellfish pan through a sieve into a bowl to get rid of any grit. Tip the liquid and shellfish back into the pan and keep warm over a low heat.

Divide the linguine among four bowls and top each one with a quarter of the shellfish and the juices.

Of course you're going to want something green to accompany all that lovely seafood. There are lots of options when it comes to the beach. Most seaweeds are edible. And there are a few more things besides...

SEA BEET

Sea beet is a member of the beet family. It grows on or above the high tide mark on most shorelines irrespective of the conditions and is rarely found anywhere else. It has spade-shaped waxy-looking leaves. The young tender leaves are the best for eating. Steam or boil them as a replacement for spinach in any recipe.

LAVER

Laver grows all over the place but it's something of a local speciality where I live on the North Devon coast. They even sell it in the local chippie deep fried in batter. Laver is a fine seaweed that can be picked at most stages of the tide because it grows throughout the tidal range. It takes a bit of effort to cook (about 4 hours if you boil it, less if you steam it) but it's one of those foods that's easy to find yet rarely eaten. One of the accepted ways to eat laver is with thick smoked bacon. Traditionally, the Welsh mix it with oats and fry it in bacon fat to make laver cakes.

SAMPHIRE

If ever you find yourself on the muddy shores of an estuary in summer, keep your eyes open for marsh samphire. It is a bright green succulent that is fabulous with any type of fish. For us, picking it is one of those family events that make eating from the wild so special. The kids can't get enough of it. And the fact that samphire thrives in mud makes it all the more fun to gather.

In some parts of the country it's possible to buy samphire at road-side stalls – for example on the North Norfolk coast where samphire is abundant. You can also buy it at some fishmongers. So if you see any, buy some to try with fish.

You can nibble the fleshiest bits straight away without cooking but most people prefer to boil it in water (unsalted) for a few minutes. Just cut off the older stringier parts and cook the tips. The taste is unique.

ROCK POOLING

Who gets the most fun out of rock pooling, me or the kids? Me probably. Despite numerous trips to the beach I still get a kick out of finding something new, unusual or endangered in rock pools around the coast.

On a recent trip to the beach we found a cuttlefish which squirted ink at me. It triggered a whole bunch of questions from the kids. There's a lot to be said for the beach being the best classroom. Every rock pool is a microcosm of the ocean, with something in it to be admired and marvelled at.

Need a little guidance? No problem. One of the best ways of seeing what's about is to go on a rock pool ramble with a qualified guide. That way you'll have someone to show you the way and to show you all the very best bits. Look online for organised rock pool rambles with any Local Authority Rangers, Wildlife Trusts and The National Trust.

The best rock pools with the most life in them will be those nearest to the low spring tide mark. Many may not seem to have much life in them at first but, since much of it will be hidden under seaweed or hiding in the darker corners, even buried in the sand, you will have to take your time and check out each pool carefully before moving on. The harder you look, the more you see. Look out for prawns, shrimps, nursery fish, crabs, starfish and anemones.

Cuttlefish

Limpet

Blennie

Starfish

BEACHCOMBING

Flotsam and jetsam galore.

Beachcombing is an age old activity. Even on the wildest days a walk along the beach looking for shells, driftwood or sea-glass can reward you with a few surprises.

All kinds of things can get washed up. Rope, old fishing nets, bits of boats, buoys, mermaid's purses, sponges. An old neighbour of mine found so much wood on one beach that he made his kitchen out of it.

Please remember that you must not take rocks, pebbles, shingle or sand. If everyone takes a few pretty stones from the beach we'll be left with no beaches! And remember that anything you find on private land (most privately owned beaches are only owned up to and including the mean tide mark in the UK) belongs to the land owner so you should ask permission first. Technically, that includes plants.

In some out of the way places a gentleman's code exists for beach foraging. Anything that has been moved above the high tide line is considered to be bagged by the person who moved it. So, if it's obviously been placed there, leave it alone, someone will be back for it later.

Plaice

Strawberry anemone

Beadlet anemone

Crab

Prawn

THE BEACHCOMBER'S CODE OF CONDUCT

★ If you spot live animals and plants, leave them be.
★ If you turn over a rock to look for something, replace it afterwards.
★ When you handle organisms, be gentle with them.
★ Be responsible about what you take from the beach. Don't take sand and pebbles.
★ Don't touch protected species.
★ If you are taking organisms for eating, only take what you need. It is illegal to take for profit without a licence.
★ Anything that looks suspicious or any 'wreck' should be reported to the Coastguard.
★ Stay clear of unstable cliffs and rock falls.
★ Always keep an eye on the incoming tide.
★ Do the beach a favour – take some rubbish with you to recycle when you go.

LOOK OUT FOR DUCKS, TURTLES, FROGS AND BEAVERS

In January 1992, 29,000 bath toys were inadvertently released back into the wild after a container fell off a ship during a wild Pacific storm. The yellow rubber ducks, red beavers, blue turtles and green frog toys were easily recognisable and their journey across the sea sparked a now famous oceanographic study into the currents of the world's oceans. Some turned up in Europe, having drifted their way thousands of miles across the Arctic Ocean. Keep your eyes peeled!

MARINE LITTER

In a recent annual Beachwatch survey the Marine Conservation Society recorded 4,700 items of rubbish per kilometre on beaches in the south west of the UK. As someone who visits the beach a lot I find that statistic really disappointing. It's too much, isn't it?

Litter kills marine life and poisons the beautiful marine environment. The sea can no longer cope with the amount of rubbish we pour in it. So why not do something about it? As well as being careful to take home all your own litter with you, why not do something very simple and very effective every time you visit the beach. Thank it by picking up a couple of bottles or pieces of rubbish that don't belong to you. Then recycle them. There you go. The world is already a nicer place.

You might enjoy taking part in a beach clean. www.beachclean.net is a good place to look for beach cleans in the South West, but they do take place all round the coast, so keep an eye out locally. Better still, organise one yourself. All you need is a few friends or family, some black plastic bags and a desire to rid the beach of its rubbish. And what better way to finish your day on the beach than by taking some food to cook over a driftwood fire and having a few beers? Go for it!!!

THE UK'S BEST BEACHCOMBING LOCATIONS

Any beach will have interesting things to find but some will have more than others. This is all to do with a combination of wind, tide, current and the weather – and geology. Beaches that are open to the elements and onshore winds (those that blow from the sea to the land) will gather more items than other, more sheltered locations. You are also more likely to find more new stuff after a storm or in places where currents trap and bring in a lot of flotsam and jetsam.

JURASSIC COAST, DEVON

The area around Charmouth on the Jurassic Coast World Heritage Site in South Devon is famous for fossil collecting. You can collect Ammonites and Bellemites right on the beach. The Jurassic Coast centre in Charmouth will show you how and will let you take home your best finds – as long as you let them know if something really special turns up. Best after bad weather and storms.

NORTH COAST, CORNWALL

The Atlantic beaches of Cornwall are the places to find old fishing nets, seaweed, driftwood and all kinds of fascinating flotsam and jetsam. Facing west into the full force of the ocean, beaches like Polzeath, Penhale Sands, Sennen Cove and Water-gate Bay are popular destinations for treasure hungry beach goers. Just get up early.

SOUTHWOLD, EAST ANGLIA

Soulthwold and Aldeburgh are famous for amber formed from the forests that once grew in the area now covered by the North Sea. After big storms you might find your very own piece of precious history. Failing that, go along and take part in the Annual Amber Hunt in August.

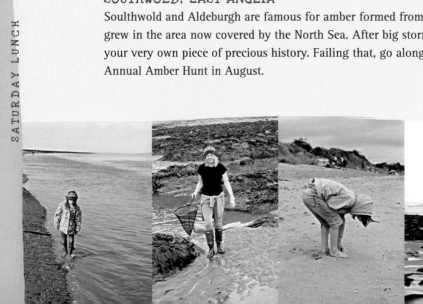

WESTERN ISLES, SCOTLAND

The Western Isles have a wild coastline with some amazing beaches that are open to the full force of the North Atlantic. The Gulf Stream brings in surprises of all kinds from all over the world. Don't be surprised to see nuts from the Caribbean or those rubber ducks from a Japanese cargo ship.

DINOSAUR COAST, NORTH YORKSHIRE

More from the last 100 millions years to find here on the beaches of North Yorkshire. Look out for dinosaur footprints and fossilised shark's teeth as well as all the usual floating debris. Best after a northerly blow and a high spring tide.

PEMBROKESHIRE, WEST WALES

The west-facing beaches of Newgale, Freshwater West, Marloes Sands and Broad Haven take everything that the Atlantic has to offer – and that includes flotsam and jetsam. Pembrokeshire has more Blue Flag beaches than any other county. All the more reason for a stop-off.

HELL'S MOUTH, NORTH WALES

Not for nothing is this fabulous beach called Hell's Mouth. It's a wild and unforgiving place that faces directly into the deep St George's Channel. But what it lacks in niceties it more than makes up for in ocean-going treasures. You might even find a beautiful piece of the fiery red semi-precious stone, jasper, which can be found here. Bring your surfboard too – it's the region's best spot for surfing.

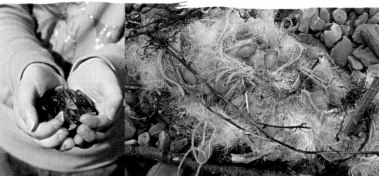

Often the best thing about foraging along the shore is just being out and about – all that sea air and seaweed. It's enough to make you hungry isn't it? Perhaps it's time to gather up your flotsam and jetsam, fill your pockets with shells and head back to the van for a spot of lunch.

CORN, BACON & parsley CHOWDER

This is quick to make and is perfect with a fresh loaf of crusty white bread. In summer fresh corn makes it all the more special.

For a fishier, more coastal flavour stir in 2 generous handfuls (about 200g) of skinned smoked haddock, cut into bite-sized chunks, when you add the corn.

FOR 4

OIL

4 RASHERS SMOKED BACON, CHOPPED

3 HANDFULS (ABOUT 150G) PEELED AND CHOPPED PARSNIP OR POTATO,
   CUT INTO BITE-SIZED PIECES

850ML MILK

1 BAY LEAF

1 X 330G TIN SWEETCORN, DRAINED (DRAINED WEIGHT 260G)

2-3 SPRING ONIONS, TRIMMED AND FINELY CHOPPED

2 TBSP CREAM

WHOLE NUTMEG, FOR GRATING (OPTIONAL)

2-3 HEAPED TBSP CHOPPED PARSLEY

CRUSTY BREAD, TO SERVE

Heat a dash of oil in a medium-sized pan and fry the bacon for 5 minutes or until crisp. Add the parsnip or potato, milk, bay leaf and 200ml water. Bring the liquid to the boil, then simmer gently, partially covered, for 20 minutes – don't venture too far away though as it will boil over easily.

Fish out and discard the bay leaf, then stir in the sweetcorn, spring onions, cream and a grating of nutmeg, and simmer for a further 5 minutes. Season to taste and stir in the parsley before ladling into bowls.

A nod to GAZPACHO

This is by no means a real gazpacho but there are similar flavours going on. If you prefer, you can use 650ml of passata rather than making your own sieved tomatoes – you might need to add a splash of water. This is a light soup to eat chilled. Follow it up with a main-course salad or the chorizo and scallop kebabs on page 153.

FOR 2 (BUT CAN EASILY BE DOUBLED OR TREBLED FOR MORE)
12 RIPE TOMATOES (ABOUT 750G)
OLIVE OIL
1 FAT CLOVE GARLIC, PEELED AND CRUSHED
2-3 DROPS TABASCO SAUCE
2-3 TSP RED OR WHITE WINE VINEGAR
PINCH OF CASTER SUGAR

TO FINISH
2 TSP EACH FINELY CHOPPED TOMATO, CUCUMBER AND RED PEPPER
1 TSP FINELY CHOPPED RED ONION
SHREDDED BASIL

Pour boiling water over the tomatoes in a bowl – leave for a minute or so, then drain, peel and chop, removing the little cores as you do so. A nice job to do sitting outside on a warm summer's morning. Tip the tomatoes into a pan with a slug of olive oil. Bring to the boil, then reduce the heat and cover. Bubble away for 15-20 minutes or until the tomatoes are very soft and have turned into a mushy sort of sauce, then leave to cool.

Sieve the cooled tomatoes into a bowl… a bit of a hassle but worth it. Stir in the garlic, Tabasco, wine vinegar, sugar and a dessertspoon of olive oil. Chill very well (overnight is ideal but not essential).

Taste to check the seasoning. Decant into bowls and top each one with a teaspoon of finely chopped tomato, cucumber and red pepper, plus a little onion and some basil.

A Spring to Summer MINESTRONE

This soup should be slurped as soon as the green vegetables are cooked. For a little meaty something, try adding shreds of dry-cured ham to the bowls before pouring in the soup. You could even stir in a little pesto.

FOR 6

OLIVE OIL

1 MEDIUM ONION, CHOPPED

1 CLOVE GARLIC, FINELY CHOPPED

6 YOUNG SPRING CARROTS

2 HANDFULS (ABOUT 100G) FINE GREEN BEANS

3 HANDFULS (ABOUT 150G) ASPARAGUS TIPS OR WHOLE SPEARS CUT INTO THREE

1.75 LITRES HOT VEGETABLE OR CHICKEN STOCK

BITE-SIZED FLORETS FROM 1 SMALL HEAD BROCCOLI (ABOUT 200G)

10 SPRING ONIONS, WHITE PART ONLY (OR TENDER BABY LEEKS,
   CUT INTO SHORT LENGTHS)

500G PEAS IN THE POD, SHELLED (ABOUT 200G), OR 3-4 HANDFULS SHELLED PEAS

1 X 410G TIN CANNELLINI BEANS, DRAINED (DRAINED WEIGHT 240G)

TO FINISH

3 TBSP EACH FINELY SHREDDED BASIL AND MINT

6 TBSP OLIVE OIL

6 TBSP GRATED PARMESAN

Heat a slug of olive oil in a large pan, add the onion and cook over a low heat for 8-10 minutes until soft, stirring in the garlic towards the end.

Meanwhile, scrub or peel the carrots and dice them. Trim the beans and cut them into short lengths. Add the carrots and stock to the pan, bring to the boil and boil, uncovered, for 5 minutes. Add the beans, asparagus, broccoli, spring onions, peas and cannellini beans. Bring back to the boil and simmer, uncovered, for 3-4 minutes or until the vegetables are just tender — don't overcook them.

While the soup is simmering, mix the shredded basil and mint with the oil, Parmesan and a pinch of crushed sea salt.

Season the soup to taste and ladle into bowls. Add a spoonful of the herb mixture to each one and stir it into the soup as you eat.

Warm QUINOA, CHICKPEA and griddled VEGETABLE salad

This is a great one for folks who like couscous but want to avoid wheat. For coeliacs it's perfect. Quinoa, incidentally, is a South American gluten-free wholegrain that was once sacred to the Incas, so if you enjoy it you'll be in good company.

This recipe can be made as a side dish or as a main meal. We tried it with slices of chorizo and loved it. But while you've got the griddle on or the barbecue going, try it with 3-4 slices of halloumi per person, drizzled with a little lemon juice and sprinkled with shredded herbs. It also makes a great salad to serve alongside fish dishes.

FOR 4

2 COURGETTES

2 RED, ORANGE OR YELLOW PEPPERS

OLIVE OIL

150G (ABOUT 210ML) QUINOA

1 X 410G TIN CHICKPEAS, DRAINED (DRAINED WEIGHT 240G)

1 TBSP RED WINE VINEGAR

2 TBSP CHOPPED BASIL OR PARSLEY, PLUS 1 TBSP MINT OR CHIVES IF YOU HAVE SOME

Trim the courgettes and slice them thinly lengthways, then quarter and deseed the peppers and cut each quarter into two lengthways. Brush the vegetables with olive oil and griddle or barbecue them for 3-4 minutes, turning, until soft and slightly charred.

Rinse the quinoa, then tip it into a pan with 350ml cold water. Bring to the boil, then reduce the heat and cook for about 15 minutes or until the grains are just tender and the water has been absorbed. Stir the chickpeas into the quinoa.

When the vegetables are ready, snip them into bite-sized pieces and toss with the other ingredients and some seasoning.

GREEK SALAD couscous

This is a substantial salad which you could eat on its own, perhaps with a handful of rocket drizzled in olive oil on the side. Otherwise, it goes well with barbecued or griddled lamb or fish.

FOR 6

200G (ABOUT 275ML) COUSCOUS
1 TBSP OLIVE OIL
QUARTER OF A CUCUMBER
2 TOMATOES
200G FETA
HALF A RED ONION
ZEST AND JUICE OF 1 LEMON
2-3 TBSP CHOPPED PARSLEY
1-2 TBSP CHOPPED MINT
SPRINKLE OF DRIED OR FRESH OREGANO (OR THYME)
HANDFUL BLACK OLIVES (OPTIONAL)

Tip the couscous into a bowl, drizzle with the olive oil and pour over 350ml boiling water. Leave to soak for 5 minutes or so. Chop the cucumber, tomatoes and feta. Peel and thinly slice the onion. Toss the couscous with these and all the other ingredients.

Chicken couscous WITH APRICOTS AND pistachios

Couscous is brilliantly versatile. You can eat it with just about anything. In this recipe, sumac – a lemony-sour Middle Eastern spice – provides a wonderful flavour. If you can't get hold of it, just use a little extra lemon zest instead. In winter, some pomegranate seeds and dates make a nice change from apricots. This is a meal in itself so it's great for picnics, but it also makes a good side dish – if you leave the chicken out – to eat with barbecued meats and fish.

FOR 4

200G (ABOUT 275ML) COUSCOUS

1 TBSP OLIVE OIL

ZEST AND JUICE OF 1 LARGE LEMON

1 TSP GROUND CUMIN

2 TBSP SUMAC

1 TBSP RUNNY HONEY

10 SOFT READY-TO-EAT DRIED APRICOTS, SLICED

1 SMALL READY-COOKED CHICKEN

2 TBSP CHOPPED PISTACHIOS (OR OTHER NUTS)

2 TBSP SESAME SEEDS

SMALL HANDFUL MINT LEAVES, SHREDDED

3 SPRING ONIONS, TRIMMED AND CHOPPED

QUARTER OF A CUCUMBER, CHOPPED

THICK NATURAL YOGHURT (GREEK IS GOOD) MIXED WITH A LITTLE HARISSA,
   CHOPPED CHILLI OR CRUSHED DRIED CHILLIES, TO FINISH

Tip the couscous into a bowl, drizzle with the olive oil and pour over 350ml boiling water. Leave to soak for 5 minutes or so. Mix the lemon zest and juice with the cumin, sumac and honey and a pinch of sea salt to make a dressing.

Take the chicken off the carcass, remove the skin and shred the meat.

Toss the couscous with the dressing and all the other ingredients. Eat topped with the spiced-up Greek yoghurt.

Caesar SALAD

Eat just as it is or toss with cooked prawns or shredded chicken. For a quick cheat's version, use five tablespoons mayonnaise, thinned with a little milk, instead of the egg yolk and olive oil.

FOR 4

2 HEADS ROMAINE (OR COS) LETTUCE

1 X 50G TIN ANCHOVY FILLETS, DRAINED AND HALVED

FOR THE CROUTONS

4 SLICES OF 1–2 DAY OLD BREAD FROM A WHITE FARMHOUSE LOAF

OLIVE OIL FOR FRYING

FOR THE MAYONNAISE DRESSING

1 LARGE EGG YOLK

1 SMALL CLOVE GARLIC, CRUSHED

2 TSP LEMON JUICE

1 TSP DIJON MUSTARD

10 TBSP (150ML) OLIVE OIL

A LITTLE MILK, IF NEEDED

2 TBSP GRATED PARMESAN, PLUS 2 HANDFULS PARMESAN SHAVINGS

FEW DROPS WORCESTERSHIRE SAUCE OR TABASCO SAUCE

First cut the bread into chunky cubes. Heat a little oil in a frying pan and fry the bread in batches until golden, adding more oil if needed. As they are ready, tip the croutons into a bowl.

For the dressing, mix the egg yolk, garlic, lemon juice and the mustard in a small bowl. Add the olive oil, drip by drip initially, mixing all the time. Once a couple of tablespoons of oil have been added, you can dribble it in, but don't stop mixing. When all the oil has been incorporated, stir in the grated Parmesan and the Worcestershire sauce or Tabasco. If the dressing is too thick, add a little milk.

Separate the lettuce leaves, shred and tip into a large bowl. Add the anchovies along with the croutons, Parmesan shavings and some freshly ground black pepper. Toss with half the dressing, add the rest and toss again; eat immediately.

A BOWL of tasty NOODLES

This is a kind of mock Pad Thai. It's pretty versatile – try replacing the prawns with cooked chicken or duck or leaving them out completely if you are a vegetarian. Sugar-snaps can be replaced with green beans or asparagus, cut into short lengths.

A good trick to avoid fiddly peanut chopping is to put the peanuts into a Ziploc bag, place that under a tea towel and then bash with a clean round rock. When you're ready to serve, open the bag and pour on. Easy!

FOR 2

150G THIN DRIED RICE NOODLES

OIL

1 FAT CLOVE GARLIC, PEELED AND FINELY CHOPPED

SMALL KNOB OF ROOT GINGER, PEELED AND SHREDDED

2 CARROTS, PEELED AND CUT INTO THIN BATONS

2 HANDFULS SUGAR-SNAP PEAS (ABOUT 100G), HALVED LENGTHWAYS

2 TBSP SESAME SEEDS

1 EGG, LIGHTLY BEATEN

2 HANDFULS SMALL PEELED COOKED PRAWNS

1 TBSP THAI SWEET CHILLI SAUCE

1 TBSP SOY SAUCE

HANDFUL OF ROUGHLY CHOPPED CORIANDER OR A MIX OF CORIANDER AND MINT

2 TBSP UNSALTED ROASTED PEANUTS, CHOPPED

Soak the dried noodles according to the pack instructions, then drain.

Heat a splash of oil in a large frying pan (or wok), and when really hot, add the garlic and ginger, stir-fry for 30 seconds. Stir in the carrots and sugar-snaps, reduce the heat to medium and stir-fry for 3-4 minutes until beginning to soften.

Stir in the sesame seeds, then push everything to one side of the pan and pour the egg into the other side. Keep the heat high-ish and as the egg begins to set, move it around to scramble and quickly mix with the vegetables in the pan along with the drained noodles, prawns, chilli sauce, soy sauce and herbs – tongs make it easier to move everything around. Toss everything together.

Eat in bowls, sprinkled with peanuts.

20-MINUTE chicken and melting CHEESE QUESADILLAS

This is a super fast lunch, supper or brunch. You can replace the chopped chillies with a drizzle of Thai sweet chilli sauce if you have some with you. And why wouldn't you? It goes with just about anything.

MAKES 4

OIL

8 SOFT FLOUR TORTILLAS

4 TBSP TOMATO RELISH, CHUTNEY OR ANOTHER FAVOURITE PICKLE

4 HANDFULS SHREDDED COOKED CHICKEN

4 TBSP GRATED CHEDDAR OR MOZZARELLA

4 SPRING ONIONS, TRIMMED AND CHOPPED

4 TSP FINELY CHOPPED RED OR GREEN CHILLI (OR USE JALAPENO CHILLI FROM A JAR)

1 LARGE JUICY LIME, CUT IN HALF

4 TBSP CRÈME FRAICHE (OR OTHER THICK SOURED CREAM)

Heat a frying pan with a drizzle of oil and, when hot, place a tortilla into the pan. Next spread a tablespoon of relish on top, then scatter with a handful of chicken, a tablespoon of cheese and a sprinkling of spring onion, chilli and lime juice. Dot with 3 teaspoonfuls of crème fraiche and place another tortilla on top. By this time the bottom tortilla should be golden, flip it over in the pan – a fish slice helps – and cook for a further few minutes or until the underside is also golden.

Slide the quesadilla on to a board, cut it into wedges and devour before cooking the next one.

whatever-you-have-to-hand PILAF

This feast is as versatile as you want it to be. The pork can be changed to chopped chicken (thighs are best) or lamb, the courgette to red pepper, the sultanas to raisins or chopped apricots and the herbs depending on what is around. Ras-el-hanout can be swapped for curry powder and the nuts add crunch but can be left out too. You can measure out the rice in your measuring jug, if you've brought one.

FOR A HUNGRY 2

2 TBSP OIL

2 THICK PORK CHOPS (ABOUT 600G), BONES, RIND AND EXCESS FAT REMOVED

1 ONION, CHOPPED

1 CARROT, TRIMMED AND CHOPPED SMALL

1 COURGETTE, TRIMMED AND CHOPPED SMALL

1 CLOVE GARLIC, FINELY CHOPPED

275ML (ABOUT 200G) BASMATI RICE

FEW PIECES PARED ORANGE OR LEMON RIND

HANDFUL SULTANAS

3 TSP RAS-EL-HANOUT MOROCCAN SPICE BLEND

570ML VEGETABLE OR CHICKEN STOCK

2 TOMATOES, CHOPPED

3 TBSP CHOPPED PARSLEY

2 TBSP CHOPPED MINT

2 TBSP CHOPPED PISTACHIOS, ALMONDS OR PINE NUTS

Chop the pork into chunks. Heat a tablespoon of the oil in a large frying pan (or shallow-sided sauté pan) and, when sizzling, brown the pork pieces until golden, then remove to a plate. Add the second tablespoon of oil and cook the onion, carrot, courgette and garlic for 4-5 minutes until beginning to soften. Tip in the rice, add the orange or lemon rind, sultanas, ras-el-hanout, half a teaspoon of salt and the pork and stir everything together over the heat for a minute.

Pour in the hot stock, give everything a stir and bring to simmering point, then cover with a tight-fitting lid and simmer for 15 minutes. Take the lid off, stir in the tomatoes, herbs and nuts and tuck in.

LEMON, PARMESAN and herb RISOTTO

Risotto is one of those brilliant camper van foods that's a big step up from beans on toast yet isn't that difficult to cook. This recipe is great as it is but you could easily add a few more bits and pieces to spice it up some more: a handful of both prawns and peas, a handful of cooked clams or mussels, some cubed gorgonzola and a handful of young leaf spinach, shredded chicken or Parma ham, blanched chopped beans or broccoli, crabmeat or crisp-fried pancetta.

FOR 4

OLIVE OIL

1 ONION, FINELY CHOPPED

2 CLOVES GARLIC, FINELY CHOPPED

350ML (ABOUT 255G) RISOTTO RICE

A SMALL TUMBLER OF WHITE WINE

1 LITRE HOT VEGETABLE STOCK

ZEST OF 1 LEMON, PLUS THE JUICE OF HALF A LEMON

LOTS OF GRATED PARMESAN

GENEROUS KNOB OF BUTTER

HANDFUL OF CHOPPED CHIVES, PARSLEY OR THYME

Heat a couple of tablespoons of oil in a large pan. Add the onion and cook for 8-10 minutes or until softened, adding the garlic for the last few minutes. Tip in the rice and stir for a good minute or so over the heat. Pour in the wine and bring to a simmer, allowing it to bubble until nearly all the wine has evaporated.

Pour in half the stock and simmer for about 10 minutes, stirring all the time, until the stock has been absorbed. Stir in the rest of the stock and continue to cook for a further 8 minutes or until the rice is 'al dente' tender but still slightly soupy.

Stir in the lemon zest and juice, 3-4 tablespoons of Parmesan, the butter and the herbs. Season and eat as soon as possible, in bowls, sprinkled with extra Parmesan.

Any sort of PASTA with ARTICHOKES, tomatoes and MOZZARELLA

There's a very good reason pasta is in your staples cupboard – because you can do almost anything with it. Try this one for something different. If cherry tomatoes aren't available, just leave them out. You could also swap the mozzarella for 2 small tins of tuna, drained and flaked, if that's more what you fancy, in which case add a couple of tablespoons of capers too. Other welcome additions are 2 tablespoons of toasted pine nuts or some chopped parsley or basil, but they are a final flourish rather than an integral essential.

FOR 4

300G DRIED PASTA (PENNE OR OTHER SHORT PASTA)

1 X 400G TIN ARTICHOKE HEARTS

2 HANDFULS CHERRY TOMATOES

OLIVE OIL

1 X 400G TIN CHOPPED TOMATOES

10 OR SO PITTED GREEN OR BLACK OLIVES, HALVED

ZEST AND JUICE OF 1 SMALL LEMON

2 GOOD PINCHES CRUSHED DRIED CHILLIES, IF YOU FANCY

1 BALL MOZZARELLA, DICED

Bring a large pan of water to the boil and cook the pasta according to the pack instructions. Drain and quarter the artichokes and halve the cherry tomatoes. Drain the pasta, then return it to the pan with a slug of olive oil, the artichokes, both types of tomatoes, the olives, lemon zest and juice, some seasoning and the chilli, if using. Heat gently together until the tomatoes begin to break up. Toss with the mozzarella and enjoy.

THAI LENTIL and coconut SOUP

A winter warmer for a cold day. You can buy Thai curry paste in small sachets so it is an easy ingredient to have on board without taking up too much space.

FOR 4-6

1 TBSP OIL

2 TBSP THAI GREEN CURRY PASTE

2 LARGE CARROTS (ABOUT 300G), PEELED AND CHOPPED SMALL

2 MEDIUM PARSNIPS (ABOUT 250G), PEELED AND CHOPPED SMALL

1 X 400ML TIN COCONUT MILK

400ML CHICKEN OR VEGETABLE STOCK

1 X 400G TIN GREEN LENTILS, DRAINED

4 GENEROUS HANDFULS YOUNG LEAF SPINACH

Heat the oil in a medium to large saucepan and stir in the curry paste, carrots and parsnips. Cook over the heat for about 10 minutes, stirring now and then. Pour in the coconut milk and stock and bring to the boil. Reduce the heat and simmer the soup, partially covered, for 15 minutes or until the chopped vegetables are just tender.

Stir in the lentils and bring back to the boil. Add salt to taste. Add half the spinach, stir until wilted, then add the other half and as soon as that has wilted, ladle into mugs or bowls.

VIETNAMESE chicken curry

This curry is mild and fresh. Thai fish sauce gives it an authentic flavour but if there is none to hand, season with salt. Eat with basmati rice.

FOR 6

4 SHALLOTS (OR 1 ONION)

THUMB-SIZED KNOB OF ROOT GINGER

4 CLOVES GARLIC

3 RED CHILLIES

OIL

1 TSP EACH GROUND TURMERIC, GROUND CORIANDER AND GROUND CUMIN

800ML COCONUT MILK

PINCH SUGAR

4 SKINLESS CHICKEN BREASTS, SLICED INTO STRIPS

2 LARGE CARROTS, PEELED, HALVED AND CUT INTO THIN BATONS

3-4 RIPE TOMATOES, SLICED INTO WEDGES

2 SPRING ONIONS, TRIMMED, HALVED AND SHREDDED

ZEST AND JUICE OF 2 LIMES

3-4 TBSP THAI FISH SAUCE

HANDFUL BASIL LEAVES, SHREDDED

SMALL HANDFUL MINT LEAVES, SHREDDED

4 HANDFULS UNSALTED ROASTED PEANUTS, CHOPPED

Peel and finely chop the shallots, ginger and garlic. Halve and deseed the chillies and finely chop them too. Heat the oil in a large pan and stir these four ingredients in, along with the turmeric, coriander and cumin. Cook over a lowish heat for 10 minutes.

Tip in the coconut milk and sugar, then bring to simmering point. Stir in the chicken and carrots and bubble away, uncovered, for 5 minutes. Stir the tomatoes and spring onions into the pan and cook for another 5 minutes. Check the chicken is cooked, then turn off the heat and stir in the lime zest and juice, Thai fish sauce and the shredded basil and mint. Taste to check the seasoning. Serve in bowls, sprinkled with peanuts.

The SURFDOTCOM Toastie

The Surfdotcom Toastie is named after an internet café Joanne and I once owned in Barnstaple. This toastie has good memories for us – and we sold thousands of them! Despite being invented for a sandwich toaster, the Surfdotcom Toastie is easy to make in the van. You'll need just a few ingredients that are readily available and easy to carry around. Remember to use a fresh loaf, as French sticks don't keep very well.

FOR 2

STICK OF FRENCH BREAD

SMALL JAR OF PESTO

2 BALLS OF MOZZARELLA, PREFERABLY BUFFALO

10 SUN-DRIED TOMATOES

OLIVE OIL SPREAD OR BUTTER

Pre-heat a griddle. Break the French stick in half. Split open the 2 halves lengthways and spread one half of each with pesto. Next, slice the mozzarella and add half to each sandwich. Scatter the sun-dried tomatoes over the mozzarella and add a few sprinkles of freshly ground black pepper.

Add the tops to the sandwiches and squash them so they are pretty much flat, then spread both sides of the outside of the sandwiches with olive oil spread or butter. Place them on the griddle pan and, keeping the heat on medium, cook for 4-5 minutes each side or until the mozzarella has melted.

A perfect post – surf snack

Pasta with SAUSAGE, FENNEL and Spinach

FOR 4

* 300G DRIED PASTA – PENNE, TROFIE OR SIMILAR
OLIVE OIL
1 ONION, CHOPPED
8 GOOD-QUALITY PORK SAUSAGES
1 TBSP FENNEL SEEDS
2 GOOD PINCHES CRUSHED DRIED CHILLIES
2 TBSP CRÈME FRAICHE OR CREAM
2 GENEROUS HANDFULS YOUNG LEAF SPINACH

Bring a large pan of water to the boil and cook the pasta according to the pack instructions. Heat a slug of olive oil in another pan, tip in the onion and fry for 5 minutes or so.

Meanwhile, squeeze the sausage meat out of the sausage skins and add to the pan (or simply add your sausages, chopped). Cook the sausage meat and onion together for 10 minutes, breaking the sausage meat up into smallish chunks as it cooks, adding the fennel seeds and crushed chillies towards the end of the cooking time.

Drain the pasta, return it to the pan and toss with the sausage mixture, crème fraiche and spinach. Eat piping hot.

SHIPSHAPE AND BRISTOL FASHION

Time for a quick scrub up before the evening begins. Talk to anyone about camper van living and they'll inevitably ask one question: "How do you wash?" It's a good question. How <u>do</u> you wash? Depending on who you are and how rugged you pretend to be, there are several answers to that question.

Some camper vans have showers. Many don't. So you can definitely forget lingering in a warm bath with soft music and mood lighting. It just isn't going to happen – unless you give up and check into a hotel. You may of course be on a well-equipped campsite with a decent shower-block, so that's easy. But otherwise you just might have to improvise a bit.

RIVERS, STREAMS, LAKES AND WATERFALLS
Next to not washing at all, this is the proper one hundred per cent hardcore way of doing things. It's quite fun but it's bloomin' cold. Bends in rivers are usually deeper and better for bathing.

The golden rule of this kind of ablution is to make sure you use eco-friendly soap or none at all. Have a splash and a quick swim but don't use anything that's not bio-degradable. Think of the fish, other wildlife, or just those downstream from you.

RIG UP YOUR OWN SHOWER
This is living! Solar showers are absolutely brilliant, pack down to nothing and can be found at most camping shops. You fill up the large black plastic container in the morning and then leave it out in the sun all day. Being black it retains the sun's heat and will warm up the water inside. Come evening time you've got yourself a nice warm shower. If you can, stand in a bucket and recycle it for the next person. Just don't be the next person. Again, make sure you use biodegradable soaps and shampoos.

TOP AND TAIL

Otherwise known as the festival freshen-up. It's the kind of wash that should be reserved for emergencies only. There's nothing nice about it – but at least you'll feel cleaner afterwards. It's better than no wash at all. Wet wipes and baby wipes, whilst they might sound like a good idea, are terrible for the environment. Avoid them if you can. Use a flannel instead.

CHECK INTO A CAMPSITE

This is the way to do it. Even if you're going to check in for just the one night and spend the rest of the time out in the wilds, a long blast of everlasting hot water will make all the difference. Use the laundry facilities whilst you're there. Take lots of fifty pence pieces. If this isn't good enough for you then maybe you should check into a hotel.

GO FOR A SWIM

Swimming pools have showers. Make the most of it. For just a couple of quid you could afford to forgo the swim and just take the shower instead. Admittedly it's not as private as it could be but when needs must it is a genuine option.

BLAG YOUR WAY IN

This is a ruse that I have tried and failed at. Maybe it's the state I'm in? But it's got to be worth a go. Find a hotel with a bar and a leisure centre. Have a drink. And then nip off for a quick shower whilst your other half watches your kit. Take it in turns, but be quick. Nobody likes getting chucked out on to the street half rinsed.

SKINNY DIPPING

Who said late-night larks can't be clean affairs? If you're going to get tipsy and lose all your inhibitions then make sure it's a skinny dip you dash for. I love to be able to cast off my clobber and make a run for the ocean. It's liberating, refreshing and, seeing as it'll be dark when you do it (I presume), no one is going to notice if you give yourself a furtive swill while you're at it. Cheap, wholesome and fun. Can't be beaten. I won't talk about my annual naked surf at Stanbury Mouth. That remains a secret.

THE UNMENTIONABLES

I am sorry but no book about camper van living is going to be complete without at least a brief mention of the unmentionables. We are going to have to break the taboo. Bears do go in the woods but there's no rule that says you have to as well. However, if you can't wait there are a few very important rules to obey.

★ If you have to go in the wild, make sure you're at least 30 metres from the nearest running water. You don't want to pollute the water course.

★ Urinate in the open where it will be diluted by rain water. Don't go in sheltered places.

★ If you need number twos, dig a hole at least six inches deep and then go. It will decompose better when covered and will pose less environmental risk.

★ If you can't dig a hole, cover it over with mulch and earth.

★ Discretion is the better part of valour. Stay away from paths and houses for goodness' sake!

★ If you can't use biodegradable toilet paper, burn it.

ON-BOARD FACILITIES

Having two kids with ants in their pants we need to be equipped for any eventuality, so we have a loo in our van. It can save a lot of bother in an emergency. When everyone else is driving around looking for the nearest public loo in a state of desperate need, we'll be alright jack. Honestly, trust me, it's a good idea, especially when it comes to festivals.

What Could Possibly Go Wrong?

Apart from being irresponsible and destroying the environment, going in the wild could make life very unpleasant for others. Whenever you can, please make use of facilities provided.

SATURDAY NIGHT

Around the campfire

Saturday night is the big night of the week. If you're lucky enough to stay at a campsite where it's ok to light a fire then you've got your evening sorted. Likewise, if you're wild camping and follow the code for lighting fires (page 130), you're good to go too. Stare into the embers and enjoy the feeling. You now have heat and light and protection.

GAZING INTO THE EMBERS

Hopefully you will also have company, because Saturday night is best when it's a social occasion. Sitting around the campfire with good friends sharing good food is a very fine thing to do. There's something about it that moves every one of us. It reminds us, as many of our camper van experiences do, of simpler times. We can toast marshmallows without a care in the world, we can stargaze, we can write our names in the air with red hot sticks the way our parents taught us, we can scan the skies for shooting stars. And we can toast our very good fortune. What else do you need?

So let's get together and talk about life, love and fun. Let's talk about the waves we caught today – and the ones we didn't catch. Let's tell stories that make us cry with laughter at our own foolishness. Let's make time for each other. Let's not watch X-Factor tonight. Let's put on our own talent show. Let's have a ceilidh.

Let's celebrate camper van living

OPEN FIRES AND CAMPING

Open fires are what it's all about. If you are new to this camper van lark, a campfire will have you hooked in no time. It is one of your fundamental needs as a camper. So I'd suggest one of the first things to look for when you're choosing your campsite is whether or not you'll be allowed to light fires. Give them a ring or look online. Try www.campfires-allowed.co.uk first.

If your campsite won't allow you to light fires then don't forget that there are plenty of places where you can. Beach fires are second to none. And no one's going to mind if you burn a few pieces of driftwood.

So you can still have your marshmallows and your late-night toast and your singalong. And I still get to tell everyone the long, yet very interesting story about the time when I was surfing and got stuck up a cliff.

Thank goodness for that.

A few things about fires I think you should know:

★ If you cook over a barbecue or light an open fire, make sure it is properly contained and that you have water or sand ready in case it gets out of control.

★ When making an open fire, dig a pit by removing a layer of turf and then line this with stones. This means you'll be able to put the turf back afterwards and that the stones will stop the fire spreading.

★ Being out in the country means making as small an impact as possible. If your fire will have a negative impact on the environment you are in, in any way whatsoever, don't light it.

★ Don't cut down trees or break off branches to light fires.

★ Don't use up all the dead wood from one area. The bugs will have nowhere to live.

★ If you are by the coast, light your fire on the beach where it will have the least impact. Use driftwood, not dead wood from forests.

★ Gather your firewood before it gets dark. Don't go scrabbling around for it after the sun has set.

Got everything together? Have you collected all the firewood you are going to need? Found the matches? Have you remembered to ask the neighbours round? Is the sun dipping towards the horizon? Good. It's time to get on with Saturday night.

THE SUN AND THE YARDARM

When you're out in the wild one of the most liberating things you can do is to throw away your watch. Not literally, obviously. But once you've got over needing to check your emails and pick up answerphone messages, the next thing to go is the need to tell the time to the hour, minute and second.

You only really need to know what time to get up (with the lark or when you feel like it), and what time you should start thinking about getting the dinner on (before the sun goes down). In between, you might want to know whether or not it is time to put the kettle on or if it is a respectable enough hour to crack open a beer, but mostly it's about making the best of the available daylight.

HOW LONG TILL SUNDOWN?

Since you might want to make sure that your bed is ready and the dinner is done well before the light fails it can be useful to know approximately how long it will be before the sun hits the horizon. You can tell this by using just your fingers. Hold your arm straight out in front of you and then turn your fingers back towards you (like in the photo). Measure how many fingers there are between the sun and the horizon. Each finger counts as (very roughly) ten minutes. Obviously there is a massive margin for error here, especially if you have sausage fingers or very short arms.

I learnt this trick from a cameraman I used to work with. If I met him again now I'd take a long look at his hands. He used this method to see how long he'd got left to film his masterpiece when we were out shooting on location. Once the sun went down, that was it – time for the crew to hit the bar after a long day in a cold and wet field.

TELLING THE TIME
WITHOUT A CLOCK

In the world before clocks, people used to be able to tell the time reasonably accurately with sundials and by approximating the position of the sun in the sky. But then again they probably didn't have meetings to go to, planes to catch or a million different things to do in a day. 'I'll see you when the cock crows' or 'meet you in the hayloft at sundown' would have been good enough.

The secret to telling the time (very roughly) without a clock is to break down the day into quadrants and work with 'solar time'. The sun is at its highest at about midday. On average it rises at about six and sets about six. If you know which way you are facing you can work it out from there. Halfway towards midday from sunrise will be 9am, halfway down will be about 3pm. Of course this will change according to the season and the location but you get the picture. Where have you got to be that's so important?

MAKE YOUR OWN SUNDIAL

Throwing your watch away might be an uncomfortable experience and telling the time from the sun might be a step too far. So why not go halfway and build yourself a very simple, home-made sundial? It's fun but don't set your watch by it, so to speak. You'll need a compass, a one metre (3ft) length of stick and 12 stones.

Firstly, work out which direction you are facing. Use the compass to determine the points. Mark north, south, east and west with a cross.

Put your stick in the ground in the centre of the cross at an angle of approximately 51 degrees (this is for the UK), or the latitude where you are, towards the north.

Then mark a semicircle with a radius of about 60cm that runs from east through north and finishes on west.

Mark north with a stone (this will be about 12 noon GMT), east with another (this will be 6pm) and west with another (this will be 6am). Divide the rest of the semicircle into sections. The rough angles of the sections are as follows (for 51 degrees latitude): 11am/1pm = 12 degrees either side of north, 10am/2pm = 24 degrees, 9am/3pm = 38 degrees, 8am/4pm = 55 degrees, 7am/5pm = 70 degrees. Use the compass to help you with the angles.

The stick should then show the approximate time with its shadow as it falls on the ground. I say approximate time because there's a lot more science to it than I could possibly include here. And it relies on the sun shining. And don't forget to adjust for BST. That said, don't rely on it to catch a plane either.

HAPPY HOUR

So now you've worked out that the hour is, in fact, respectable enough to open the drinks cabinet, it's time to get out the camper van cocktail shaker. In our case that's a jam jar. They are useful for all sorts of things besides holding jam and collections of nails. I use them for mixing salad dressings and shaking cocktails. Who needs all that fancy shaking, muddling and mixing stuff? Not us.

JAM JAR MOJITO for a Summer's day

The mojito may have started as a pirates' drink and is a brilliant way to get in the swashbuckling mood.

MAKES 1 GLASS
12 MINT LEAVES
3 TSP SUGAR
HALF A LIME, CUT INTO 2 WEDGES, PLUS 2 TBSP LIME JUICE
4 TBSP RUM
ICE
50-75ML SODA WATER

Put the mint leaves and sugar into a jam jar. Add the lime wedges and squash them, in the jar, with the end of a spoon – do this for a good minute or so to muddle the ingredients together and release the flavours. Add the lime juice and rum. Put on the lid and give everything a good shake. Pour over ice in a glass and top up with soda water.

JAM JAR whisky mac for a WINTRY EVENING

When there's a definite nip in the air, this whisky mac will warm you from the inside out.

MAKES 1 GLASS
2 TBSP WHISKY
2 TBSP GREEN GINGER WINE
1 PIECE PARED LEMON RIND

Put all the ingredients into a jam jar and gently swirl together. Pour into a small glass or cup and sip slowly.

Cheers!

Martin's BLOODY MARY

Every time I have a Bloody Mary it reminds me of Sunday lunches in the pub and outdoor parties on hot summer days. It's a good feeling, filled with the first flushes of lazy afternoon sessions and balmy nights under the stars. Bloody Marys have been made many ways over the years by all kinds of famous chefs and 'mixologists' but my way is pretty simple and effective. That's because I prefer the slapdash approach: chuck it all in and hope for the best. To do this, however, you need to start somewhere.

Best drunk over ice, Bloody Marys make a very nice ease-in-to-the-sundowner session. They're spicy and fresh and ever so slightly alcoholic, unless you slip, in which case they are very alcoholic.

MAKES 4 TALL GLASSES
1 TBSP CREAMED HORSERADISH SAUCE
2 TBSP WORCESTERSHIRE SAUCE
DASH OF TABASCO SAUCE
JUICE OF 1 LIME
1 LITRE CARTON TOMATO JUICE
200-300ML VODKA
ICE CUBES
HANDFUL OF CORIANDER LEAVES
CELERY SALT

Spoon the horseradish into a jug. Pour on the Worcestershire sauce, the Tabasco and the lime juice. Season with a little freshly ground black pepper. Mix it up, then add the tomato juice and mix it some more.

Pour in the vodka, add a handful of ice cubes (if you have them). Mix it a little more then pour into glasses. Garnish each glass with a few torn coriander leaves and a dusting of celery salt.

Sarah's JAM JAR
Bloody Mary

Another take on this cocktail classic. Try both versions, and have a great evening.

FOR 1

200ML PRESSED TOMATO JUICE (FROM A CARTON)

2 TBSP VODKA

1 TBSP DRY SHERRY

1 TSP WORCESTERSHIRE SAUCE

1/2 TSP LIME (OR LEMON) JUICE

5 DROPS TABASCO SAUCE

SHAKE OF CELERY SALT

TO FINISH

3-4 ICE CUBES

CELERY STICK

Shake everything in a jam jar, then tip it into a glass. Finish with a few ice cubes and a celery stick.

MULLED CIDER with orange and cloves

Sometimes as the sun goes down it can get a little chilly. So why not offer your camping companions something warm to wrap their mitts around? This mulled cider will do the job nicely.

FOR 4

2 MUGFULS CIDER (ABOUT 500ML)

2 MUGFULS APPLE JUICE (ABOUT 500ML)

3 TBSP BRANDY

1 ORANGE, HALVED AND EACH HALF STUDDED WITH CLOVES

FEW PIECES PARED LEMON RIND

2 CINNAMON STICKS

3 TBSP SOFT BROWN SUGAR

1 EATING APPLE, CORED AND SLICED

Heat all the ingredients together in a pan. Bring to the boil, then gently simmer for at least 15 minutes. Pour into heatproof cups or mugs.

A jug of PIMM'S for a CROWD

If you're going to invite the neighbours round, do it properly. This recipe for Pimm's should seal the deal. Just make sure you ask them to bring their biggest jug. You're going to need it. This recipe includes borage, a very pretty blue-flowered hedgerow herb that is traditionally added to Pimm's, but if you can't find it don't worry – it's just as good without.

FOR 10 WITH TOP-UPS

2 HANDFULS MINT LEAVES

1 LEMON, SLICED

1 SMALL ORANGE, SLICED

HALF A CUCUMBER, HALVED LENGTHWAYS, THEN SLICED

2-3 HANDFULS STRAWBERRIES, HALVED

PLENTY OF ICE

1 X 70CL BOTTLE PIMM'S

LARGE BOTTLE GOOD-QUALITY LEMONADE

LARGE BOTTLE GINGER ALE

SPRIGS OF BORAGE (OPTIONAL)

Divide the mint, lemon, orange and cucumber slices and the halved strawberries among two or three jugs. Add a generous handful or two of ice to each one.

Add half or a third of the Pimm's to each jug and top up with two parts lemonade and one part ginger ale. Finish by adding a few sprigs of borage.

Give everything a quick stir and leave the ice to do its work for 15 minutes. Before you know it, it'll be Pimm's o'clock.

BEEF POT ROAST
in a DUTCH OVEN

A Dutch oven is a heavy, cast-iron casserole (and the lid often doubles up as a frying pan) which is perfect for campfire cooking as it retains heat incredibly effectively. If you fancy buying one, Sarah's recommended Dutch oven is the Lodge Logic Dutch oven, made by Lodge Cast Iron Manufacturing Co. Check out www.lodgemfg.com; they're also available from www.kitchenmonger.co.uk.

If you prefer, leave the potatoes out and tuck some potatoes, wrapped in foil, into the fire embers, to bake in their jackets. Chunks of peeled parsnip, swede or squash are a nice addition to the pot roast, as is a handful of dried ceps (porcini) added at the same time as the carrots and potatoes. Either way, eat with lots of crusty bread on the side.

FOR 4

4 ROUNDED TBSP PLAIN FLOUR

1KG BEEF TOPSIDE

OIL

500ML RED WINE

500ML BEEF STOCK

3 TBSP TOMATO PURÉE

1 TBSP REDCURRANT OR QUINCE JELLY

200G SMOKED BACON LARDONS

FEW SPRIGS FRESH THYME OR ROSEMARY

3 OR 4 BAY LEAVES

2 STRIPS PARED ORANGE RIND

8 SHALLOTS, PEELED (AND HALVED, IF LARGE)

4 CLOVES GARLIC, PEELED BUT LEFT WHOLE

3 HANDFULS (ABOUT 250G) CHANTENAY CARROTS, OR SAME QUANTITY REGULAR CARROTS, SCRUBBED AND CUT INTO 5CM LENGTHS

3 HANDFULS (ABOUT 200G) SMALL NEW POTATOES, HALVED

Tip the flour into a shallow dish and season well with crushed sea salt and freshly ground black pepper. Roll the beef in the flour until it is covered all over. Heat a splash of oil in the Dutch oven (or in a regular flameproof casserole) and brown the piece of beef all over until crusty and golden, then transfer it to a plate.

Add any flour left in the dish to the Dutch oven and pour in the wine and stock. Stir in the tomato purée and the jelly and bubble for a few minutes. Return the beef to the casserole and scatter the lardons, herbs, bay leaves, orange rind, shallots and garlic around the beef. Bring the liquid to simmering point (do this on the hob if it takes too long over a campfire) then cover the Dutch oven with a tight-fitting lid and place on a grill over a campfire or in the embers (or even on the hob) to simmer for an hour, turning the beef every 20 minutes.

Tip in the carrots and potatoes, cover again and simmer for a further 30 minutes, or until everything is tender.

FIRE-BAKED sea bass with leeks, samphire and TARRAGON

Sea bass, the fisherman's nemesis. Well, mine anyway. I have been on so many trips to try and catch sea bass that it's getting silly now. No. Off to the fishmonger's again.

If samphire isn't available use sprue asparagus, asparagus tips or fine green beans instead. They will only need 4-5 minutes' cooking.

FOR 4

2 WHOLE PREPARED, CLEANED SEA BASS, BREAM OR SNAPPER, EACH ABOUT 750G

2 LEMONS, ONE SLICED AND THE OTHER JUICED

2 CLOVES GARLIC, THINLY SLICED

8 BAY LEAVES

OLIVE OIL

SMALL KNOB OF BUTTER, PLUS 1 TBSP

4 LEEKS, TRIMMED AND THINLY SLICED

2 SMALL TUMBLERS OF DRY WHITE WINE OR VERMOUTH

4 GENEROUS HANDFULS SAMPHIRE (SEA ASPARAGUS)

2 TBSP CHOPPED TARRAGON LEAVES (OR PARSLEY, CHIVES, DILL OR CHERVIL)

Slash the skin of each sea bass on both sides. Season the inside and outside of each fish with sea salt and freshly ground black pepper. Tuck lemon and garlic slices and bay leaves inside the fish cavities and drizzle lemon juice into each one.

Cook the fish on a grill over a campfire (or on a barbecue) in a barbecue fish basket for 20-30 minutes, turning halfway – the timing will depend on the heat of your fire and size of the fish. Alternatively, wrap each fish in a parcel of foil or greaseproof paper and a couple of sheets of thoroughly dampened newspaper. If you want to cook the fish in the embers, wrap them in a double layer of oiled kitchen foil – just watch out for burnt fingers!

Heat a generous slug of olive oil with the knob of butter in a fireproof frying pan alongside the fish and cook the leeks for 8-10 minutes or until soft. Pour in the wine or vermouth and bubble until there are only a couple of tablespoons left in the pan. Stir in the samphire, cover and steam cook for 3-4 minutes. Take the lid off, stir in some freshly ground black pepper, the tablespoon of butter and the tarragon – you won't need any salt as samphire is salty. Serve alongside the sea bass.

BAKED APPLES, the
campfire way

Pudding. A must for some. You can do this recipe in your Dutch oven or in the embers of the fire. To cook them the campfire way in the embers, stuff the apples with the fruit, nuts and zest, then wrap them individually in a double layer of foil, dotting them with butter and adding a little honey, orange juice and apple juice as you go. Either way, eat the hot apples with crème fraiche, Greek yoghurt or custard. If you prefer you can use only sultanas.

FOR 8

8 EATING APPLES

4 TBSP CHOPPED OR SNIPPED READY-TO-EAT DRIED FIGS

2 TBSP CHOPPED OR SNIPPED STONED DATES

4 TBSP SULTANAS

3 TBSP HAZELNUTS OR PECANS, CHOPPED

2 ORANGES

200ML APPLE JUICE (OR CIDER)

3 TBSP RUNNY HONEY (OR GOLDEN SYRUP)

GENEROUS KNOB OF BUTTER

Core the apples using, preferably, a corer, or a small, sharp knife until you have a nice-sized cavity in each one. Score around the centre of each apple to prevent them from bursting as they cook. Put the apples into the Dutch oven (or a flame-proof casserole).

Mix the dried fruit and divide among the apple cavities, scattering any excess around the apples. Scatter the chopped nuts over the top. Zest the oranges over the apples, then squeeze the juice and pour that over the apples, along with the apple juice. Drizzle over the honey and dot each apple with butter.

Bring the liquid to simmering point (you can do this on the hob if it takes too long over a campfire) then cover with a tight-fitting lid and simmer the apples over a campfire (or on the hob) for 20 minutes or until tender. Ideally, transfer the cooked apples to a dish and reduce the juices over the heat until syrupy before drizzling them back over the fruit.

A SPOT OF EVENING FISHING

What I don't know about fishing could fill a library. Literally. I am really, really bad at it. But I really love it. This is probably because whenever I catch a fish, which I do from time to time, it's a massive thrill and keeps me on a high for a day or two. For someone like me, who has been desperately trying to find their inner hunter-gatherer, it is also confirmation that I am capable and have a place in the world. My family, who should be proud and praise me for my manliness and cunning, remain, as ever, unimpressed.

Besides, it's nice to stand on a rock doing something largely mindless with nothing for company but the sea, a rod and (very rarely) a few fish. On occasions when I do catch anything it's straight into the pot for a meal that's absolutely delicious.

Catching your very own supper

145

MACKERS and MASH,
camper van STYLE

Shallow-frying in garlic and butter is one of my favourite ways to cook mackerel – especially straight out of the sea – letting the rich, oily flesh do its own good work.

Be warned. It could be prudent to cook the fish outside the van. Mackerel can stink up the neighbourhood a bit. Not seriously, but enough to hang about on the upholstery for a while.

FOR 4

8 LARGE POTATOES (KING EDWARDS OR SIMILAR)
PINCH OF CRUSHED DRIED CHILLIES
MUGFUL PLAIN FLOUR
8 MACKEREL FILLETS
BUTTER
OLIVE OIL
1 CLOVE GARLIC, SLICED
ABOUT 1 TBSP EACH WHOLEGRAIN MUSTARD AND CREAMED HORSERADISH SAUCE
2-3 TBSP OF MILK
4 LARGE HANDFULS (ABOUT 300G) SPINACH

Put the spuds on to boil. Meanwhile, in a bowl, mix the crushed dried chillies, a pinch each of ground black pepper and sea salt and the flour. Lightly coat each mackerel fillet in the seasoned flour. When the spuds are almost done, put a knob of butter, a splash of olive oil and the garlic in a frying pan and gently heat together to melt the butter. Scoop the garlic out of the pan, then fry as many mackerel fillets as you can fit into the pan in one go flesh side down on a high heat for a couple of minutes. Turn and cook the skin side for another few minutes until golden. If necessary melt a little more butter and oil, then fry the second batch.

Drain the spuds (but try to save some water for the steamer) and mash them roughly with a fork. Add the mustard, horseradish, two large knobs of butter and a generous splash of milk. Mash again until the texture is 'rustic'. Lastly, steam the spinach until wilted, then toss with a little olive oil and season. Serve up in a pile, starting with a dollop of mash, followed by a layer of spinach and with the fillets on top. Garnish with a smile, watch the sun go down and thank your lucky stars you remembered the washing-up liquid.

ONE-PAN MACKEREL with onion, capers and SULTANAS

When I cooked this mackerel dish of Sarah's, it stole the show. The salty taste of the capers with the sweetness of the sultanas and the rich fishy flesh was just beautiful.

This is definitely one for the beach. Or you could even turn it into a meal with some cooked and sliced new potatoes. Pile them on to the plates before topping with the onions and fish. If you get lucky more than once, to ring the changes, replace the capers and sultanas with a rounded teaspoon of ras-el-hanout Moroccan spice blend – mix it with the onions before you return them to the pan.

A SNACK FOR 4 OR A MEAL FOR 2

2 RED (OR BROWN) ONIONS

OLIVE OIL

4 MACKEREL FILLETS, SKIN ON

3 TBSP RED (OR WHITE) WINE VINEGAR

1 TBSP CAPERS

2 TBSP SULTANAS

Peel, halve and thinly slice the onions. Heat a little oil in a frying pan and cook the onions in it until soft, about 10 minutes. Score the skin of the mackerel fillets.

Tip the cooked onion into a bowl. Add a dash more oil to the pan and cook the mackerel fillets skin side down over a highish heat for 3-4 minutes or until the skin is lightly golden. Carefully turn the fillets over and sprinkle with sea salt and freshly ground black pepper.

Return the cooked onions to the pan along with the red wine vinegar, capers and sultanas. Let everything bubble together for a few minutes, then tuck in.

A stewy kind of SEAFOOD SOUP with CHILLI, fennel and orange

If you haven't managed to catch your own mackerel you might want to use different fish – and buy it from the fishmonger. Remember to make sure what you buy is sustainably sourced or responsibly farmed. This recipe is good eaten with some grilled French bread spread with garlicky parsley butter. If passata is hard to get use tinned chopped tomatoes instead.

FOR 6 AS A STARTER (OR 4 AS A MAIN)

- 1 RED PEPPER
- 1 SMALLISH BULB FENNEL
- 1 STICK CELERY
- 1 LEEK
- 2 TSP OLIVE OIL
- 2 CLOVES GARLIC, FINELY CHOPPED
- 700G PASSATA (CRUSHED TOMATOES)
- 2 PIECES PARED ORANGE RIND
- 1 TSP CRUSHED DRIED CHILLI
- 3 LARGE HANDFULS HADDOCK FILLET OR OTHER FIRM-FLESHED WHITE FISH (ABOUT 450G), CUT INTO BITE-SIZED CHUNKS
- 3 HANDFULS (ABOUT 200G) SHELLED MEDIUM TO LARGE RAW PRAWNS
- 6 HANDFULS (ABOUT 750G) CLEANED AND PREPARED MUSSELS
- 2 HEAPED TBSP CHOPPED PARSLEY OR CORIANDER

Halve and deseed the pepper, then slice into strips and cut the strips into smallish pieces. Trim and chop the fennel into similar-sized chunks and do the same with the celery. Trim the leek, then halve lengthways and slice each half quite thinly.

Heat the oil in a large pan and add all the vegetables and the garlic. Cook over a gentle heat, covered, for 15 minutes until softened, stirring occasionally.

Pour in the passata and 400ml of water then stir in the orange rind, chilli and half a teaspoon of salt. Bring the soup to the boil. Tip in the fish, prawns and mussels, then put the lid back on and simmer everything for a further 10 minutes. Stir in the parsley or coriander, then ladle into deep bowls to serve, discarding any mussels that haven't opened during cooking.

THE BBQ

Ladies, take a step back. This is man stuff. The barbecue is, and always will be, the domain of the Alpha male. In surfing circles, this fine specimen would be known as Fistralian Man. Amusing pinny, devil-may-care ways, cocked chef hat, cocksure attitude, cold beer, hilarious stories. What could possibly go wrong?

It's such a cliché but somehow it always happens. And not without reason, legitimate or not. Man (like the fool he is) is drawn to fire. It's just one of those things. As soon as the sun comes out, in gardens across the UK, overweight and balding men will mobilise. Thanks to their annual culinary skills they will single-handedly – but not without encouragement from the Beta males in the troop – save their family from certain starvation by burning a couple of frozen burgers and incinerating half a dozen sausages. More likely than not these will still be uncooked in the middle.

All I can say is, thank goodness 'er indoors has got the chicken drumsticks in the oven already – it'll be dark in three hours. Oh, hang on. Wait a minute. There is no indoors. You're on your own now soldier. Better get used to it.

And anyway, thankfully, Sarah's BBQ recipes are easy – and delicious.

Helpful hints for men who already know how to light a BBQ

(and don't need help but might like to keep it handy anyway in case things go pear-shaped and they need to rescue the situation before anyone notices)

★ Disposable barbecues are handy but evil. That's because they are massively wasteful and the people who use them leave them on the beach where I live. It makes me a bit cross. Better to become familiar with your very own portable BBQ and its charming idiosyncrasies.

★ Gas barbecues are for the amateur garden enthusiast. It's cheating. Real men don't use them. Convenience is not your friend.

★ Bucket barbies are neat, and easy to store in your van.

★ Briquettes will last longer than charcoal. One-touch bags won't last very long at all.

- ★ Store your charcoal in a dry place. That way it will light more easily.

- ★ Build your BBQ with a pyramid of coals interspersed with firelighters. Once it is lit, spread the coals out so they are reasonably even but do leave an area where you can keep food warm.

- ★ Don't start cooking until the charcoal or briquettes have a layer of ash on them and have stopped flaming.

- ★ Don't cook near flammable items. Don't say I didn't warn you.

- ★ If something starts to flame (because of fat) move it out of the flame. If you squirt it with water it will cause ash to get on the food.

- ★ Don't be tempted to use WD40 on your BBQ if it isn't lighting properly. It looks impressive to the other males hanging around but isn't really the answer. Besides, it's dangerous. Better to start again.

SCALLOP and chorizo KEBABS

Scallops are a real treat and we love them. While I have yet to go diving for them (that's the only sustainable way to have them) and doubt I ever will, a trip to the fishmonger is all the excuse I need to grab a few. This recipe also works well with large, peeled prawns instead of scallops.

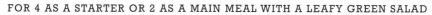

FOR 4 AS A STARTER OR 2 AS A MAIN MEAL WITH A LEAFY GREEN SALAD
12 LARGE SUSTAINABLY-SOURCED SCALLOPS – WITH OR WITHOUT THE ROE
12 CHUNKY ROUNDS (ABOUT 110G) CHORIZO
1 LEMON – HALF CUT INTO 4 CHUNKS AND THE OTHER HALF CUT INTO WEDGES
1-2 TBSP FRESH THYME LEAVES

If using wooden skewers, soak them in cold water for 30 minutes before using to prevent them from burning. Otherwise, use metal ones. Fire up the BBQ or use a griddle if you're in a no-fire zone.

Alternate scallops and rounds of chorizo on 4 skewers, adding a lemon chunk to each one to finish.

Barbecue for 5-6 minutes or until cooked through, turning now and then. Transfer the kebabs to a plate, sprinkle with the thyme and a little sea salt. Serve the wedges of lemon alongside to squeeze over as you eat.

MONKFISH kebabs with lemon CAPER DRESSING

Makes a simple supper for two. You can cook these on a griddle or on the barbie and all you need is four long skewers. If you use wooden ones soak them first in cold water for 30 minutes. Absolutely delicious with couscous, rice or some good bread to mop up the juices. With a glass of Pimm's and a roaring driftwood fire, who wouldn't love this?

FOR 2

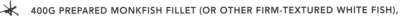

400G PREPARED MONKFISH FILLET (OR OTHER FIRM-TEXTURED WHITE FISH),
   CUT INTO 16 CHUNKS

8 SLICES DRY-CURED HAM, SUCH AS PARMA HAM, HALVED

2 LEMONS

6 CHESTNUT OR WHITE MUSHROOMS, HALVED

4 TBSP OLIVE OIL

2 TBSP CAPERS

Wrap each chunk of monkfish in half a slice of ham. Cut one of the lemons into eight chunks. Thread a chunk of lemon, a piece of ham-wrapped fish and half a mushroom on to a skewer. Thread ham-wrapped fish pieces and mushroom pieces on to the skewer in turns, so that you have four pieces of fish separated by three mushroom halves. Repeat with the other three skewers and finally add another chunk of lemon to the end of each one. Fire up the barbecue (or griddle).

   Cook the kebabs for 10-12 minutes, turning them now and then until tinged golden. Mix the juice of the other lemon with the oil, capers, a pinch of sea salt and some freshly ground black pepper. Drizzle over the cooked kebabs.

BARBECUED LAMB with orange, garlic and HERBS

This also works really well with a whole shoulder of lamb. Use about 1.6kg to serve 4, but remove the bone from it before marinating.

FOR 4 WITH SECONDS

1 WHOLE BONELESS LEG OF LAMB, WEIGHING ABOUT 1.25 KG, AT ROOM TEMPERATURE

2 ORANGES

1 BULB GARLIC

LEAVES FROM 2-3 SPRIGS FRESH ROSEMARY, CHOPPED

LEAVES FROM 2-3 SPRIGS FRESH THYME

2 TBSP DIJON MUSTARD

Using a sharp knife, make five or six small slashes on both sides of the piece of lamb. Put the lamb into a large bowl and add the zest and juice of the oranges. Peel and crush the garlic cloves and add to the bowl along with the rosemary, thyme, mustard and some freshly ground black pepper.

Using your hands, mix all the marinade ingredients together and rub them all over the lamb. Cover and leave to marinate for a few hours (or overnight if you can wait that long).

Fire up the barbecue. Barbecue the lamb over a medium heat for 20 minutes, then turn it and barbecue the other side for 20 minutes; this is a rough guide as barbecues vary so much in temperature but this usually produces lamb that is charred on the outside and still pink in the middle. Once cooked, leave the meat to rest for 15 minutes off the heat. Slice to serve and sprinkle with a little crushed sea salt.

LAMB BURGERS with spring onions and FETA

You can't go camping and not have a burger. It's the rules. But in our book it says that burgers must also be made fresh. Spice lovers can add a pinch of crushed dried chillies if they fancy.

MAKES 4

500G LAMB MINCE

3 SPRING ONIONS, TRIMMED AND FINELY CHOPPED

4 TBSP CHOPPED MINT OR CORIANDER (OR A MIXTURE OF BOTH)

1 HEAPED TSP GROUND CUMIN OR CORIANDER

GENEROUS PINCH GROUND CINNAMON (NOT ESSENTIAL)

1 MEDIUM EGG, LIGHTLY BEATEN

2 RIPE TOMATOES

HALF A SMALL RED ONION

8 TBSP THICK NATURAL YOGHURT, SUCH AS GREEK

SQUEEZE OF LEMON JUICE

8 SLICES FETA

4 LARGE BURGER BUNS OR WRAPS

HANDFUL OR TWO OF SALAD LEAVES

In a bowl, break up the mince with a fork, then sprinkle over the spring onions, half the herbs, the cumin or coriander, cinnamon and some seasoning. Mix together, then add the egg and mix again. Don't overwork the mixture or the burgers will be tough.

Form the mince into 4 balls and transfer to a large plate or board, then flatten them slightly into burgers. Chill for 30 minutes. Fire up the barbecue (or a griddle). Slice the tomatoes and peel and slice the red onion. Mix the yoghurt with the rest of the herbs and a squeeze of lemon juice and season.

Cook the burgers for 4-5 minutes on each side. Spread each bun or wrap with a spoonful of herby yoghurt. Tuck a burger, a couple of slices of feta and a few slices of tomato and red onion into each bun or wrap. Add a sprinkle of sea salt, another spoonful of herby yoghurt and a few salad leaves to finish.

Barbecued RIB-EYE with BRUSCHETTA and CHUNKY hazelnut SALSA

If you don't want to indulge yourself with one large piece of rib-eye, then you could always go for a couple of good-quality, good-sized rib-eye steaks. Cook them on a hot barbecue for a few minutes each side so that they are still lovely and pink in the middle.

The flavours of the salsa are based on Spanish romesco sauce – gutsy and delicious.

FOR 4 GENEROUSLY

 1KG PIECE RIB-EYE STEAK, AT ROOM TEMPERATURE

4 HANDFULS (ABOUT 200G) ASPARAGUS TIPS, OR SAME QUANTITY WHOLE SPEARS,
  CUT INTO THREE

8 SLICES SOURDOUGH OR CIABATTA BREAD

OLIVE OIL

FOR THE SALSA

4 GENEROUS TBSP BLANCHED HAZELNUTS

8 RIPE TOMATOES, CHOPPED

4 CLOVES GARLIC, PEELED AND FINELY CHOPPED

2 TSP SMOKED SWEET PAPRIKA

2 GENEROUS PINCHES CRUSHED DRIED CHILLIES

2 TBSP RED WINE VINEGAR

5 TBSP OLIVE OIL

Fire up the barbecue. For the salsa, toast the nuts in a frying pan until lightly golden. Leave to cool.

Barbecue the meat over a medium heat for 40 minutes – this is a rough guide as barbecues vary so much in temperature but this should give you meat that has a crusty dark exterior and a rare pink centre. Continue cooking if you prefer the meat medium-well done. Once cooked, leave the meat to rest for 15 minutes off the heat.

Meanwhile, barbecue the asparagus and the slices of bread on both sides (you may need to put the asparagus on a piece of foil if the bars of the grill are wide). Arrange the slices of bread on a large platter or board, drizzle with a little olive oil and sprinkle with sea salt.

To finish the salsa, chop the nuts and mix in a bowl with the tomatoes, garlic, paprika, chillies, vinegar, olive oil and two pinches of sea salt – you don't want to mix everything too far ahead as you want to keep the crunch of the hazelnuts.

Spoon half the salsa over the bread and scatter the asparagus over the top. Slice the beef and arrange the slices over the salsa and asparagus. Spoon the rest of the salsa over that. Let everyone dig in and help themselves. Or for individual servings, see the picture below.

Eat there and then

COUSCOUS on the side

Another simple and quick side dish to accompany grilled or barbecued meats or fish. Or adapt to suit… a handful of crispy chorizo or bacon, some chopped toasted nuts, some chopped ripe tomatoes are all good to add, or in the winter replace the beans with cubes of pan-fried butternut squash.

FOR 4

200G (ABOUT 275ML) COUSCOUS

1 TBSP OLIVE OIL

1 TSP HARISSA PASTE

3 HANDFULS RUNNER BEANS OR GREEN BEANS, CUT INTO SHORT LENGTHS

4 HANDFULS CHOPPED PARSLEY

ZEST OF 1 LEMON, PLUS JUICE OF HALF A LEMON

Bring a pan of salted water to the boil. Tip the couscous into a bowl, drizzle with the oil and pour over 350ml boiling water. Stir in the harissa and leave to soak for 5 minutes or so. Boil the beans for 2-3 minutes until just tender, then drain.

Fluff up the couscous with a fork, stir in the parsley, lemon zest and juice and the beans. Mix everything together and add sea salt to taste. Eat warm or cold.

PASTA on the SIDE

This is full of lovely summer flavours. Use it to accompany grilled or barbecued steak or fish. In the winter, you could adapt this by using one 400g tin of chopped tomatoes instead of fresh, 3 tablespoons of chopped thyme instead of basil, the zest of a clementine instead of lemon and adding a handful of capers or sliced olives – warm through before tossing with the pasta.

FOR 4

 200G DRIED PENNE OR OTHER SHORT PASTA

6 RIPE TOMATOES

COUPLE OF PINCHES CRUSHED DRIED CHILLIES

2 CLOVES GARLIC, CRUSHED

GENEROUS HANDFUL TORN BASIL LEAVES

ZEST OF 1 LEMON

OLIVE OIL

Bring a pan of salted water to the boil and cook the pasta according to the pack instructions. Roughly chop the tomatoes, removing the small cores at the top of each one as you do so. Tip into a large bowl and stir in the chillies, garlic, basil, lemon zest and a splash of olive oil.

Drain the cooked pasta and leave to cool for 5 minutes or so then tip into the bowl with all the other ingredients and add crushed sea salt to taste. Eat warm or cold.

STEAMED summer vegetables with HERBS

Steaming veg is marvellous. The results taste better and are much better for you than boiled veg. Steaming is easy too. You just add a couple of inches of water to the pan, pop the veg on top and let it steam away for a few minutes. Including herbs adds a little extra zing.

You can serve steamed veg with just about anything: cold cooked chicken, griddled fish, red meat. In our van the steamer is essential equipment. Try it with chunks of root vegetables and squash in the winter. Rosemary, thyme and parsley will add a wholesome herby flavour that's hard to beat. Just lovely.

FOR 2

2 BAY LEAVES (NOT ESSENTIAL)

6 SMALL NEW POTATOES (ABOUT 150G) HALVED, OR 8 BABY TURNIPS

8-10 BABY SPRING CARROTS OR ABOUT 150G STANDARD CARROTS CUT INTO BATONS

8-10 BABY LEEKS OR ABOUT 75G STANDARD LEEKS CUT CHUNKILY

2 HANDFULS ASPARAGUS TIPS (ABOUT 100G) OR 6-8 WHOLE SPEARS, HALVED

KNOB OF BUTTER OR 1 TBSP OLIVE OIL

3 TBSP CHOPPED HERBS, E.G. TARRAGON, MINT AND CHIVES OR CHERVIL,
   BASIL AND PARSLEY

1/2 TSP ORANGE, LEMON OR LIME ZEST

Bring a pan of water to the boil, adding a couple of bay leaves to the water if you have them. Put your steamer on top of the pan. Scrub and trim the vegetables as necessary. Tip the potatoes and carrots into the steamer and cook for 10 minutes – make sure the water is boiling all the time and top it up with more boiling water should it run low. Next, add the leeks and asparagus and continue steaming everything together for 4-5 minutes or until tender.

Take the steamer off the pan, tip out the cooking water (or save it for using as vegetable stock when making soups) and tip the cooked vegetables into the pan with the butter or oil, the herbs, zest and some seasoning. Toss together over the heat for a minute or so, then devour.

BROCCOLI, pine nut and CHILLI salad

Green is good. And with a bit of chilli to give it a kick you're going to love it. This salad is just as tasty with purple sprouting broccoli and is equally delicious warm or cold. As with all recipes, go for a pinch of crushed dried chillies if you can't get your hands on the fresh stuff. If you fancy a change, it's delicious mixed with hot pasta and a touch of grated Parmesan cheese too.

FOR 4

3 TBSP PINE NUTS

1 HEAD BROCCOLI, ABOUT 400G

500G PEAS IN THE POD, SHELLED (OR ABOUT 200G/3-4 HANDFULS SHELLED PEAS)

2 TBSP OLIVE OIL

1 RED CHILLI, DESEEDED AND FINELY CHOPPED (OR A PINCH OF CRUSHED DRIED CHILLI)

Toast the pine nuts in a pan over a medium heat for 3-4 minutes or till golden. Tip on to a plate. Add water and a pinch of salt to the pan and bring to the boil. Discard the bulk of the broccoli stalk and cut the rest of the broccoli into florets.

Add the broccoli florets to the pan. Bring back to the boil and simmer for 4-5 minutes, adding the peas for the last minute, then drain both.

While still warm, toss the broccoli and peas with the toasted pine nuts, olive oil, chilli and a pinch of sea salt.

FRESH and GREEN
lemony salad

This recipe is a good one to have to hand when it's your turn to be chef during roadside roulette. Courgettes, cucumbers, broad beans? Come the summer time, makeshift roadside stalls will be overflowing with them. If you can't find broad beans, you can improvise with fine green beans cut into short lengths.

FOR 4

2-3 COURGETTES

HALF A CUCUMBER

500G BROAD BEANS IN THE POD, SHELLED (OR ABOUT 150G/2 HANDFULS SHELLED BROAD BEANS)

2 TBSP OLIVE OIL

ZEST OF 1 LEMON AND JUICE OF HALF A LEMON

150G NATURAL YOGHURT

GENEROUS HANDFUL CHOPPED OR TORN FRESH HERBS – A MIXTURE OF BASIL, SNIPPED CHIVES AND MINT IS A GOOD CHOICE

Bring a pan of water to the boil. Trim the courgettes and cut them and the cucumber into thin batons. Add the broad beans to the boiling water, bring back to the boil and simmer for 3-4 minutes, then drain.

Mix the courgettes and cucumber in a large bowl with a generous pinch of sea salt, the olive oil and the lemon zest and juice. Leave aside for 15 minutes. Remove the outer white skins of the broad beans and toss them with the rest of the salad, the yoghurt and herbs, then eat soonish.

Mart's SALAD dressing

The best thing about this salad dressing is that you can shake it up in a jam jar, keep it in the van and use it whenever you like – all you have to do is shake it up. Stored in a cool cupboard it should last for a few days. It's great with any leaf salad and has a nice herby and garlicky hit. Add it to a plain leaf salad or to tomatoes and mozzarella. You could even try it with fresh broad beans and spring onions.

ENOUGH FOR 4

2 CLOVES GARLIC
FEW SPRIGS FRESH ROSEMARY
1 TSP WHOLEGRAIN MUSTARD
1 TSP RUNNY HONEY
BALSAMIC VINEGAR
OLIVE OIL
SESAME OIL (IF YOU HAVE IT, BUT NOT ESSENTIAL)

Peel and finely chop the garlic and rosemary and place both in a jam jar. Next, spoon in the wholegrain mustard, honey and a pinch of black pepper and sea salt. Pour in two fingers of balsamic vinegar, then two and a half to three fingers of olive oil – tasting it as you go. Add just a dash of sesame oil if you happen to have some.

Next, screw the lid on and shake the lot up. There you are – salad dressing on the go.

Simple SLAW

A great one for roadside roulette. What self-respecting roadside stall isn't going to have carrots and cabbage? Exactly. This makes loads but it'll keep for a day if chilled.

FOR 8

4 CARROTS
HALF A WHITE CABBAGE
8 TBSP (250ML) NATURAL YOGHURT
1 TBSP WHOLEGRAIN MUSTARD
3 TBSP GOOD-QUALITY BOUGHT OR HOME-MADE MAYONNAISE

Scrub the carrots – there is no need to peel them unless they are very dirty – then grate them and tip into a large bowl. Cut the cabbage half into two quarters and thinly shred, then add this to the grated carrot. Mix together the yoghurt, mustard, mayonnaise and some seasoning and tip into the bowl with the vegetables. Toss together to mix.

Now then...
   any room for pudding?

Lemon cup CHEESECAKES

A zesty lemony pud to wake up the senses. Tasty too.

FOR 4
JUICE OF 1 LEMON, PLUS A LITTLE ZEST
5 TBSP ICING SUGAR
150ML DOUBLE CREAM
200ML THICK NATURAL YOGHURT, SUCH AS GREEK
4 GINGER BISCUITS
4 TBSP RASPBERRIES, BLUEBERRIES, HEDGEROW BLACKBERRIES OR CHOPPED
   STRAWBERRIES (OR NO FRUIT AT ALL)

Dissolve the icing sugar in the lemon juice. Whip the cream to soft peaks and mix with the Greek yoghurt and the lemon mixture.

Crumble a ginger biscuit into the bottom of each of four cups (or glasses), followed by a spoonful of fruit in each. Top with the lemon mixture and sprinkle some lemon zest on top. Chill for an hour or so before eating.

A SPRING to Summer FRUIT fool

If you want to make a sort of Eton mess, crumble a couple of individual ready-made meringue nests into the mix. If gooseberries are not to hand, try rhubarb or soft summer berries – summer berries will only need 5 minutes' cooking with a sprinkling of sugar until their juices run.

FOR 6

450G GOOSEBERRIES, TOPPED AND TAILED

3 TBSP ELDERFLOWER CORDIAL (OR A DASH OF WATER)

4 TBSP RUNNY HONEY

200ML DOUBLE CREAM

300G BOUGHT, READY-MADE FRESH CUSTARD

ELDERFLOWERS, WHEN AVAILABLE, OR LEMON ZEST

Tip the gooseberries into a pan with the cordial or water and the honey, bring gently to a simmer and cook over a low heat, partially covered, for 15 minutes, then leave to cool completely.

Mash the gooseberries to a purée, then drain in a sieve over a bowl. Tip the collected juices into a small pan and bubble to reduce to a couple of tablespoons.

Whip the cream to soft peaks, then mix with the custard and the mashed gooseberries. Pile into cups or glasses. Drizzle each one with a little of the reduced syrup and sprinkle with elderflowers or lemon zest before tucking in.

sticky TOFFEE PECAN apples

A nip in the air? Keep your shorts on but slip on a chunky jumper and a beanie and enjoy this quick pudding fix. Try it with slices of banana or plum too.

FOR 4

1-2 TBSP CHOPPED PECAN (OR OTHER) NUTS

LARGE KNOB OF BUTTER

4 EATING APPLES OR PEARS, CORED AND CUT INTO WEDGES

GENEROUS SLUG OF CALVADOS, ARMAGNAC OR DARK RUM

2 TBSP LIGHT OR DARK SOFT BROWN SUGAR

1-2 TBSP DOUBLE CREAM, PLUS EXTRA FOR GREEDY EATING

Toast the nuts in a frying pan until golden, then tip into a bowl and leave to cool. Heat the butter in the pan and, when foaming, add the apples or pears. Cook for a couple of minutes, turning – you want the fruit to start to soften. Turn the heat up high, add the booze and bubble everything away for a minute or so.

Sprinkle the sugar and a small pinch of salt over the fruit and stir together to make a toffee-ish sauce. Finish by stirring in a slosh of cream. Sprinkle with the chopped toasted nuts, and eat hot with chilled cream on the side.

CAMPFIRE MUSIC

Every campfire needs a camp guitarist. Without a singalong to rouse the rebels in our hearts even the biggest and best-made campfire can seem a little empty. It's like having a sleepover without ghost stories or camping without a camper van. It's good, but somehow things aren't quite right.

What better way to see in the wee hours than sitting around the glowing embers singing songs that make you feel great, bring a tear to your eye or stoke the fire in your soul? No one cares if you can't hold a tune. No one cares if it's a bit naff. The important part is being there, in the moment. The next most important thing is that you sing something everybody knows.

As an amateur and very average campfire guitarist I know how quickly a fireside gathering can turn. One minute you're singing your own misty-eyed composition about the girl from the fruit shop, the next everyone's looking at their shoes and kicking the embers in embarrassed silence. Then they go to the pub. The moral? Give them what they want. Don't make the campfire your testing ground for new material – unless you want to be singing to yourself that is.

Here are a couple of guitar songs that are really easy to play with just a few chords. If you are already an accomplished musician, you might want to look away now.

DRUNKEN SAILOR

Sea shanties. Brilliant. Who cares if you've heard it a thousand times before? The reason it's a classic is because... it's classic. Everyone knows the words and people who can't sing can shout. Something for the folk singer inside all of us.

VERSE 1

Am
What shall we do with a drunken sailor?
G
What shall we do with a drunken sailor?
Am   C G   Am
What shall we do with a drunken sailor, earlye in the morning?

CHORUS

Am
Hooray and up she rises!
G
Hooray and up she rises!
Am   C G   Am
Hooray and up she rises, earlye in the morning.

VERSE 2

Put him in a longboat till he's sober...

VERSE 3

Dip 'im in the drink until he's sober...

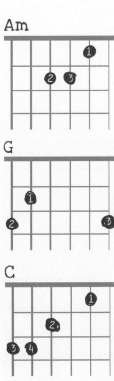

THE JOHN B SAILS

My father-in-law, Ed Quill, and his best mate, Tommy Radley, sang this beautiful
song on my wedding day – in the bar, after most of the other guests had gone home.
Rightly so. It's emotional stuff all right but should be sung with joy in your heart.
We'll have none of that crying in your pint round our campfire thank you.

VERSE 1

C
We come on the sloop John B, my grandfather and me.
                              G
Around Nassau town we did roam.
             C   F
Drinkin' all night. Got into a fight.
              C   G   C
Well, I feel so break up, I want to go home.

CHORUS

C
Hoist up the John B's sails. See how the main sails set.
                                    G
Call for the captain ashore, let me go home.
                C   F
Let me go home. I want to go home.
              C   G   C
Well, I feel so break up, I want to go home.

VERSE 2

First mate, he got drunk. Broke up the people's trunk.
Constable had to come and take him away.
Sheriff John Stone, why don't you leave me alone?
Well, I feel so break up, I want to go home.

VERSE 3

Well, the poor cook he caught the fits. Throw away all of my grits.
Then he took and he ate up all of my corn.
Let me go home. I want to go home.
This is the worst trip since I've been born.

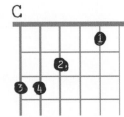

C

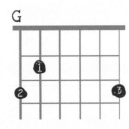

G

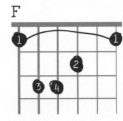

F

COOKING MARSHMALLOWS OVER AN OPEN FIRE

Anyone got any marshmallows? They are the perfect accompaniment to any musical accompaniment, if you see what I mean, and are one of camping's guiltiest pleasures. Bring out a bag of these pink and fluffy monsters and you'll be hailed a real hero at the next cook-out. Not only will you be providing an easy distraction from the singing but you'll also be giving everybody back a favourite little bit of their childhood. It's magical stuff.

TOASTING IS EASY

Stick a marshmallow on a long pointy stick and heat it over the flames until the outside is caramelised and the inside is all gooey. Eat. Are you loving it? Oh yes...

CABIN FEVER

After all that lovely food and music, let's take the tempo down a bit. Sometimes reality bites and the heavens open. So what happens when it's been raining all day, you're wet and miserable, supper is over and the pub is a very long walk away? It's a long, long time until bedtime isn't it? You might find you are going ever so slightly insane.

In case you haven't experienced this before, this is cabin fever. It can strike even the hardiest of hardcore campers. Thankfully there are plenty of things you can do to alleviate the boredom. And they needn't cost a fortune.

LEARN SOME SIMPLE MAGIC TRICKS

Magic isn't my forte but I can fool the kids with a few playing cards and a bit of cheap sleight of hand if I absolutely have to. I'm not talking rabbits and top hats here, just a pack of playing cards. To be honest I could do with a book to tell me how to do it better. That would absolutely amaze them – and take up some of the very long hours until bedtime when you've got no TV.

RAIN RAIN GO AWAY

CUP STACKING

You've seen this on the internet haven't you? It can be absolutely amazing to watch someone stack a load of paper cups at a hundred miles an hour. It's surprisingly difficult. Give it a go. You could be the next world champion.

MAKE UP STORIES

When you're in a dark and lonely field it might not be ideal to scare each other with ghost stories but other tales will do. Try 'My Dad bought a VW camper van. In it he had... an accident'. Start with A and work your way through the alphabet repeating each one and adding another as you go. If you get as far as Q, use quinoa. There's a recipe for it on page 106 so it'll be at the back of the cupboard already.

GET THE GAMES OUT

If you've followed my advice you will have packed up a few board games, playing cards and pastimes in your top locker. Now is the time to get them out. Snakes and ladders, checkers, chess, backgammon. There's no end of Victorian-style fun to be had.

GET A LAPTOP
WITH A VERY LONG BATTERY LIFE

What? You thought camper van living was all about whittling sticks and making hammocks? It might be when it's sunny but sometimes you might just need to pull something truly astounding out of the hat. The laptop with DVD player. It's our dirty little secret weapon of mass entertainment.

If none of this works for you, put on your waterproofs, wind up the lantern and go to the pub.

Any camper van outing can only be enhanced by a trip to the pub. It's another natural part of the whole experience. And sometimes it's a chance to dry out and enjoy a snifter before bedtime. But for goodness' sake, take a torch. It's dark out there in the country. Really dark.

Sometimes a trip to the pub can save a bad trip from being the worst trip ever. If tension is high and the rain is falling, a couple of stiff drinks will sort it out. Of course, once you've gone all the way there and all the way back you're going to be a little peckish. No problem. Our back-from-the-pub grub is just what you need.

CHEESY eggy BREAD

Crunchy bread and melting cheese, all in one bite. A helpful night-before-the-morning-after hangover cure. Highly recommended. And actually highly recommended for a light lunch snack too.

FOR 2

 1 LARGE EGG LIGHTLY BEATEN WITH 2 TBSP MILK
SOFT BUTTER
THICKLY SLICED WHITE BREAD, FROM A FARMHOUSE LOAF
GRATED CHEDDAR
OIL

Tip the egg mixture into a shallow bowl or dish and season. Butter the bread and make cheese sandwiches, then cut each sandwich into two or four, depending on the size of your slices.

Heat a knob of butter and a splash of oil together in a frying pan. Dip both sides of the sandwich halves or quarters in the eggy mixture to coat well. Fry for a few minutes on each side until the bread has formed a rich, golden crust and the cheese has melted. Devour.

Stroopwafels

These delicious Dutch, waffle-shrouded biscuits of toffee loveliness are something else. Apparently the recipes for them are closely guarded by mothers and bakeries alike. The traditional way to eat them is to leave them on top of your cuppa for a few moments so that the caramel inside starts to melt a little. They are simply divine. You can buy them all over the UK and Ireland so if you see them, buy them: they are often called toffee or syrup waffles. Our friend Marieke used to get them from her Dutch relatives and bring them to us. A real treat.

On their own stroopwafels are good, but with crème fraiche and a few fresh strawberries or hand-picked blackberries they are a post-pub snack to die for. Heat 'em up on your cuppa, dollop on your crème fraiche, pile on the fruit and, hey presto! A perfect snack.

PEANUT BUTTER and bacon SANDWICHES

The sweetness of peanut butter combined with salty crispy bacon and soft white bread makes for a fine sarnie at any time of the day, but when you've had a few it's manna from heaven.

BACON (2-3 RASHERS PER PERSON)
SOFT BUTTER
THICKLY SLICED WHITE BREAD, FROM A FARMHOUSE LOAF
CRUNCHY PEANUT BUTTER

Fry the bacon until crisp. Meanwhile, butter the bread and spread with peanut butter. Top with the rashers of hot bacon, add another slice of bread on top to make a sandwich and squash slightly with the flat of your hands. Leave for a minute or so to allow everything to melt and mix. Enjoy.

FESTIVALS AND FESTIVAL LIVING

I've been to a few festivals. Not many, but enough. They can sometimes be grubby experiences. But it doesn't have to be that way. If you are heading to a festival this year then it is absolutely imperative that you take your van. If you don't have one then rent one (more about this on page 270) or beg, borrow or steal one. You will not regret it.

When you are at a festival your camper will really come into its own. There might be a sea of mud outside but inside the van you will have your privacy, somewhere comfortable to sit, somewhere dry to shelter, somewhere to cook and wash, some-where to hide if it all gets too much and – best of all – you will have your own sweet space when all around is chaos. If you have friends with vans and get there early enough to bag a decent spot you can create your very own corral. A few wind breakers will set it off nicely and an awning will give you wet weather space and storage. Once you're in and settled there will be nothing to stop you from having a wild old time.

WHAT'S YOUR FESTIVAL FANCY?

There are now so many festivals in so many shapes and sizes. You can go for the big name events like Glastonbury or Reading or go smaller and more intimate at music events like Solfest in Cumbria. Some will be more family-friendly than others so choose carefully if you are going with kids.

Basically, when it comes to festivals, it's whatever takes your fancy. Live a little. You can listen to folk music, drool over classic VWs, thumb through a few books, see carnivals and parades, rave the night away or check out the world's greatest bands on the biggest stages music has to offer.

For a few of the less mainstream and more unusual festivals, see our festival listings on page 274.

TOP TEN FESTIVAL TIPS

Choose carefully. There are so many festivals that it can be hard to know where to start. Intimate festivals are great but it could mean there's not much to do if you've got kids with you. On the other hand, big festivals can be daunting for some.

Get there early. That way you won't have to park on a slope or by the main thoroughfare or in the last spot next to the toilets.

Take an awning. This will double your space and makes a top spot for civilised dining.

Take a porta-potti. You might have to go in the awning when nature calls but at least you won't have to queue for hours and face the horror of festival loos. Take paper.

Stack your cooler with ingredients. Unless you like eating chips, mung beans and falafels you should consider cooking for yourself at least once a day.

Go with friends. That way you'll be able to create your own mini camper village. Meet up and go in convoy.

Take levelling chocks. If the ground isn't absolutely level you might have to jack up the van a little. Chocks help.

Take face paint. The easy way to get into the hippy vibe. Slap on a little warpaint.

Take a flag on a very long pole. This will make your home enclave easier to spot. You won't miss your vans in a sea of vans and tents.

Take a bottle of champagne. I don't care what anyone says, this is the way to do it. Live the life. Last time we were at a festival Martin and Cath brought out a bottle to have with our first dinner, the Vietnamese curry on page 119. It felt glorious to have a taste of the good stuff when all around was anarchy. And you get to say things like "The band are on? Gimme a mo to chug this Bolly and I'll be right there with you."

Big Chill CHILLI

It's Saturday night and the neighbours are coming round before they head off to catch the headliners, so you'll need something to keep things hot and spicy for the night ahead. This is just perfect. It'll take a little time to make but it's worth it. If you can't spare the time, do the shorter version, using mince, which is equally delicious. There is one thing for certain though: you're going to need a big pan. And if you've got the whole campsite coming round, you're going to need two pans. Perhaps even a friendly neighbour to help you cook the rice.

Eat with rice or griddled flatbreads and a spoonful of holy moley guacamole on the side (see page 186). This is great for kids if you serve it in wraps with sour cream. Just wrap 'em up and send them off (but go easy on the chilli).

FOR 8-10

(IF YOU WANT TO COOK THIS FOR 4 OR 5 PEOPLE, SIMPLY HALVE THE QUANTITIES)

 2 LARGE ONIONS, CHOPPED

2 CLOVES GARLIC, CRUSHED

OIL

1.25KG STEWING STEAK, CUT INTO SMALL CUBES, OR BEEF MINCE

2 TSP SWEET SMOKED PAPRIKA

2 TSP HOT CHILLI POWDER

2 TSP GROUND CUMIN

1 TSP GROUND CINNAMON

3 TBSP TOMATO PURÉE

2 X 400G TINS CHOPPED TOMATOES

2 RED PEPPERS, DESEEDED AND CHOPPED INTO SMALLISH CHUNKS

2 X 410G TINS RED KIDNEY BEANS, DRAINED (DRAINED WEIGHT 480G)

2 SQUARES GOOD-QUALITY DARK CHOCOLATE

3 TBSP ROUGHLY CHOPPED CORIANDER LEAVES

FINELY CHOPPED RED CHILLI (OR SLICED CHILLIES FROM A JAR), SOURED CREAM AND
  LIME WEDGES, TO SERVE

Using a big pan, cook the onions and garlic in a couple of tablespoons of oil over a low heat for 8-10 minutes or until softened. Scoop on to a plate. Turn the heat up.

Add the meat in batches and cook until browned, transferring it to a plate as it's ready, then return it all to the pan with the onions and garlic, the spices and tomato purée, stirring well.

Add the tinned tomatoes, red peppers and a generous pinch of salt. Fill one of the empty tomato tins with water and add that too. Bring to the boil, then reduce the heat and simmer, covered, over a low heat. If using stewing steak, simmer the chilli for 1 hour 15 minutes, adding the beans and removing the lid after 45 minutes (check the meat is tender and continue to cook for a little longer if not). If using mince, simmer the chilli for 1 hour, adding the beans and removing the lid halfway.

Check the seasoning. Stir in the chocolate to melt and add richness, followed by the coriander. Serve with bowls of chopped or sliced chilli, soured cream and lime wedges – to add if you wish – with holy moley guacamole alongside.

HOLY MOLEY guacamole

This zingy, fresh guacamole goes perfectly with the Big Chill chilli. It'll cool you down if things get a little hot but then spice them up again – with its very own tangy zip.

   Like the Big Chill chilli this is for a crowd – but it doesn't have to be. Halve the quantities if there are fewer of you or double them if you're expecting more.

FOR 8-10 WITH THE CHILLI

3-4 RIPE TOMATOES

3 LARGE, RIPE AVOCADOS

PINCH CRUSHED DRIED CHILLIES OR SWEET SMOKED PAPRIKA

ZEST AND JUICE OF 1 LIME

3 TBSP ROUGHLY CHOPPED CORIANDER LEAVES

Peel and chop the tomatoes. Peel and de-stone the avocados, then mash in a bowl. Add the chopped tomatoes, chilli, lime zest and juice, coriander and a pinch of salt.

LAMB, aubergine and Spinach CURRY

To avoid a multitude of spices, use a ready-made curry paste to make this mild aromatic curry. Tuck in with a few poppadoms, some griddled naan bread or rice.

FOR 8

OIL

1–1.2KG WHOLE BONELESS LEG OF LAMB, TRIMMED OF EXCESS FAT, CUT INTO CHUNKS

2 AUBERGINES, TRIMMED AND CUT INTO QUARTERS AND THEN CHUNKS

2 ONIONS, CHOPPED

4 CLOVES GARLIC, CHOPPED

1 TSP SALT

1 X 283G JAR MEDIUM ROGAN JOSH CURRY PASTE, PATAK'S OR SIMILAR

2 X 400G TINS CHOPPED TOMATOES

1 CINNAMON STICK

5-6 HANDFULS (250G) YOUNG LEAF SPINACH

3-4 TBSP CORIANDER LEAVES

NATURAL YOGHURT AND CHOPPED, DESEEDED GREEN CHILLI, TO FINISH

Heat a tablespoon of oil in a very large pan and when sizzling, brown the lamb over a high heat, in batches, transferring it to a bowl as it is ready.

Heat another tablespoon of oil and brown the aubergines, in two batches, transferring them to the bowl as they are ready. Add more oil as you need it.

Reduce the heat and cook the onions in a little more oil until they are really soft, 15 minutes or so. Stir in the garlic, salt and curry paste and cook for another few minutes.

Return the browned lamb and aubergines to the pan along with the tinned tomatoes and cinnamon stick. Fill one of the tomato tins with water and add that too. Stir and bring to the boil, then reduce to a simmer and bubble away, partially covered, for 1 1/2 hours. Skim off any excess oil that gathers on the surface.

Just before eating stir the spinach into the curry – add it handful by handful and as soon as it has wilted, stir in the coriander and serve. Spoon into bowls and top with yoghurt and chopped green chilli.

Moroccan VEGETABLE tagine

Another fabulously tasty – and remarkably easy – dish for 10 of your best friends. A few of these ingredients will need to be sourced before you head off but needless to say they are worth having on board. Ras-el-hanout and harissa (both sold in small sachets or pots) are great standbys to add to couscous and meat or fish stews. This dish should be eaten with couscous – 500g soaked in 750ml boiling water and 4 tablespoons of olive oil will be the right amount. To finish, toss the soaked couscous in a pan with some melted butter and toasted chopped almonds.

FOR 10

OLIVE OIL

3 ONIONS, CHOPPED

4 CLOVES GARLIC, FINELY CHOPPED

5 TSP RAS-EL-HANOUT MOROCCAN SPICE BLEND

1 LARGE BUTTERNUT SQUASH (OR SIMILAR), PEELED AND CUT INTO CHUNKS

4 LARGE PARSNIPS, PEELED AND CUT INTO CHUNKS

2 AUBERGINES, TRIMMED AND CUT INTO QUARTERS AND THEN CHUNKS

2-3 GENEROUS PINCHES SAFFRON STRANDS

3 X 400G TINS CHOPPED TOMATOES

JUICE OF 1 LEMON

2 TBSP HONEY

4 ROUNDED TSP HARISSA PASTE

1 TSP SALT

5 COURGETTES, TRIMMED, CUT INTO CHUNKS AND THE CHUNKS HALVED

12 PITTED SOFT, READY-TO-EAT DATES (ABOUT 100G), ROUGHLY CHOPPED

4 PRESERVED LEMONS, FINELY CHOPPED AND PIPS REMOVED (OR ZEST OF 2 LEMONS)

5 TBSP CHOPPED CORIANDER AND 2 TBSP CHOPPED MINT, MIXED

Heat a generous slug of oil in a very large pan (or casserole) and cook the onions in it, over a gentle heat, for 10 minutes. Add the garlic and ras-el-hanout and stir together over the heat for another minute or so. Tip in the butternut squash, parsnips, aubergine and another slug of oil. Give everything a good stir and, when sizzling, cover and cook gently for 10 minutes.

Stir in the saffron, tomatoes, lemon juice, honey, harissa and a teaspoon of salt. Bring everything to simmering point and cook, covered, for 25-30 minutes, adding the courgettes, dates and a cup of water halfway through.

Once all the vegetables are tender, spoon into bowls and sprinkle with preserved lemon and the mixed chopped herbs.

SUNDAY MORNING

The morning after
the night before

Today is going to be the day of all days. After a great Saturday night you're going to need something pretty special to top it off. An unusual sport. A bit of excitement. An adrenaline fix. Why not? Put on your adventure trousers and try something new.

A BREAKFAST FIT FOR ADVENTURE

In our house the 'day of all days' is still a day to remember. We were lucky to have had the experience. The fun began with a sailing taster session at the Tamar Lakes in North Cornwall. It was something we'd wanted to do for a long time – to learn how to travel under sail. Perhaps it's the start of a bigger dream. We'll see.

It was a gorgeous summer day with a light breeze. Despite capsizing my dinghy three times (once intentionally) we walked away with our certificates and headed for the beach. There, still in our wetsuits, we swam in the sea. Then it was back to the van for lunch, a beer and a snooze. By this time the breeze was a whisper so I went surfing whilst Joanne read the papers. To finish off the day we had a barbecue on the beach and went to the pub. Brilliant. When I think about it now, I feel a smile creep across my face.

Everyone should have a day of all days in their life. It's not so difficult to achieve, especially when you're in the van. You can go anywhere and do anything you want. Just set the coordinates for somewhere you like the sound of and drive. Don't stop until you've gorged yourself on new experiences.

So, what's on the menu for today? Where would you like to go? What have you always wanted to do? What will make you smile in the days and years to come? What will make your heart sing?

Then do it.

But first, you're going to need a hearty breakfast. A breakfast that's fit for adventure.

TOAST

I tend to gush over a lot of stuff but toast is one staple that truly deserves it. I can't get enough of it. There was a time – during a period of less enlightened living – when I almost lived on toast. I wasn't even a student at the time. There is as much toast as there is bread, which is why, to a gastro-toaster like me, there is a whole world of toasting opportunity out there.

And let's not get on to toppings.

For me it's salted butter and Marmite on a hefty wholemeal. Or is it peanut butter on thick sliced white? Raspberry jam and clotted cream on a farmhouse doorstep? Who knows? They are all equally delicious and can and should be eaten at any time of the day or night. Don't let anyone tell you otherwise.

CAMPER VAN TOASTING METHODS

ON THE COOKER: Camping shops sell toasters that work on the gas ring in the van. They take four slices and are pretty good, though, like a domestic grill, you still have to remember to turn the toast over to do both sides. Also, don't forget to let the toaster cool down before you take it off the gas ring. Obviously they are designed to get very hot. Don't say I didn't warn you.

UNDER THE GRILL: It's too simple isn't it? Chuck the bread under the grill, turn once, eat. If your van has a grill, that is.

PAN TOASTING: This is a bit more like camping. Lightly butter the bread and then cook it in a pan either on a very high heat on the gas ring, or over an open fire. It's kind of like a fried slice but not quite so greasy.

OVER AN OPEN FIRE: Great if you are out in the wild. You'll need a toasting fork to stop your mitts from burning. They are easy enough to make. Get a metal fork and lash it to a long piece of driftwood (don't use plastic or flammable string, a piece of wire is best). Hold it over the fire, turn it over and hey presto, toast! It can be a bit smoky and can fall off the fork, so watch out.

Double-handed
BREAKFAST BANJO

What a name! It must be good. Well actually it is, but it can be a little messy, hence the banjo part of the title (see Exploding Egg Banjo, page 54, for full details) and the fact that you'll need both hands to eat it. This is a way to enjoy a hearty Full English but without too much washing-up as it's a one-pan affair. Why waste time at the sink when you could be out there having fun?

As usual I would opt for dry-cured, thick-sliced back bacon from local pigs and free-range eggs from local hens, if available. A slice of juicy beef tomato helps to keep it feeling fresh and healthy (just).

FOR 2

2 RASHERS DRY-CURED BACK BACON

2 LARGE MUSHROOMS

OLIVE OIL

1 BEEF TOMATO

2 FRESH FREE-RANGE EGGS

2 FRESH PLAIN BAGELS

MAYONNAISE, TO SERVE

Fry the bacon and the mushrooms in a little olive oil for a few minutes until both are cooked the way you like them. Slice the tomato. Remove the bacon and mushroom from the pan and fry the eggs in the remaining oil. Meanwhile, slice the bagel and toast lightly on both sides under the grill.

To serve, put the bacon in first, then the mushroom, then the egg and finally, the tomato. Grind a little black pepper on to the tomato and then drop a dollop of mayonnaise on top. Replace the top of the bagel. Serve with fresh orange juice and a hot cup of tea. Be careful it doesn't explode all over your pyjamas.

PORRIDGE with cinnamon and RAISINS

Wild camping in the Highlands? Nae bother. This tasty porridge will get you up in the morning all right. Save it for a cold and frosty morning to get the very best out of it.

FOR 4

2 MUGFULS PORRIDGE OATS (ABOUT 200G)

2 TSP GROUND CINNAMON

HALF A MUGFUL RAISINS

1 LITRE MILK, PLUS A LITTLE EXTRA

SOFT BROWN SUGAR

Tip the oats into a pan and stir in the cinnamon and raisins. Add the milk and stir again, then bring everything to simmering point. Once the porridge is bubbling, turn the heat to low and gently cook the porridge for 4-5 minutes or until creamy and thickened.

Spoon into bowls, top with a drizzle of extra milk and a generous sprinkling of brown sugar.

Fresh fruit for BREAKFAST

Who doesn't love fresh fruit for breakfast? But instead of the old favourites, why not try something different? A few fresh herbs can make it – try shredded basil or mint on these.

FOR 4
HALF A MUGFUL ORANGE OR APPLE JUICE
GENEROUS TBSP OR SO SHREDDED BASIL OR MINT (OPTIONAL)
YOGHURT AND HONEY, TO SERVE

FOR SUMMER
2 HANDFULS HULLED AND HALVED STRAWBERRIES
3 HANDFULS RASPBERRIES
3 HANDFULS BLUEBERRIES
2 PEACHES OR 4 APRICOTS, STONED AND SLICED

FOR WINTER
1 PINK (OR WHITE) GRAPEFRUIT, PEELED AND SLICED
2 ORANGES, PEELED AND SLICED
1 LIME, PEELED AND SLICED
2 KIWI FRUIT, PEELED AND SLICED
1 SMALL MANGO OR PAPAYA, DE-STONED, PEELED AND SLICED

Mix the fruit with your juice of choice and the basil or mint if using. Pile into bowls and top with yoghurt and a drizzle of honey.

PANCAKES for breakfast

Are you hungry? Great. Go for these pancakes. They can be made in minutes and are delicious straight from the pan.

MAKES ABOUT 10

THREE-QUARTERS OF A MUGFUL (ABOUT 100G) PLAIN FLOUR

2 LARGE EGGS, LIGHTLY BEATEN

275ML MILK

3 TBSP (ABOUT 50G) BUTTER, MELTED AND COOLED SLIGHTLY, PLUS EXTRA FOR COOKING

SUGAR AND LEMON, TO SERVE

Sift the flour into a largish bowl with a pinch of salt. Make a well in the centre and add the eggs. Pour the milk and melted butter into the well too and thoroughly whisk everything together. The resulting batter should be the consistency of double cream.

To cook the pancakes, melt a small knob of butter in a frying pan and swirl it around to coat the base – ideally the pan should be no bigger than 18cm in diameter (or make fewer, larger pancakes).

Add 3 tablespoons of batter to the hot pan and immediately tilt the pan so the batter runs and covers the surface. Cook for a minute or so, then flip over and cook the other side. Continue until all the batter is used up, adding more butter as needed. Eat the pancakes scattered with sugar and a squeeze of lemon juice (and then folded or rolled) or try them with…

. . . a drizzle of honey and a squeeze of fresh orange juice

. . . a light sprinkle of ground cinnamon, a generous drizzle of maple syrup
  (or golden syrup or treacle) and a scattering of blueberries

. . . a good smear of hazelnut chocolate spread (Nutella) followed by a
  handful of toasted, chopped pecans

. . . a dollop of soured cream and a spoonful or two of chopped crispy fried bacon
  and sweetcorn

HIT THE SURF

The surf lifestyle and the camper van lifestyle are almost inseparable. Surfing gives you a destination and a purpose. When you've got waves on your mind you have somewhere to go, a reason to put your foot down and drive. As the conditions change and the surf changes with it, so you can pack up and ship out to somewhere better. Did surfers invent the gap year? Probably. For the rest of us, who get it in bite-sized chunks at the weekend or on holiday, surfing gives us a very good reason to get up in the morning. And the van gives us the means to live well while we're there.

Of all the sports I have tried over the years, surfing is simply the best, hands down, no contest. There is something about catching waves that is absolutely magical. It could be about being in harmony with nature and experiencing the power of the ocean. It could even be about escapism, being cool, dropping out or living for the moment. Personally I think it's about nothing other than pointless, mindless fun. Brilliant, brilliant fun. But whatever it is, once you've mastered gliding down the face of a clean, crisp ocean roller, there is no going back. Not ever. Believe me when I say that surfing has the power to change people's lives.

SURFING EQUIPMENT

You don't need much to be able to surf. Just a board and a wetsuit, a few lessons and a lot of time to perfect your moves. Naturally, as you get more into it you'll need boots, gloves and a hat for winter surfing, a board bag, a good pair of shorts, some flip-flops, a whole new wardrobe, lots and lots of money for petrol and maybe even flights to hot places.

But let's start with the basics:

★ Surfboards come in many different sizes and shapes, and there will be one out there that's perfect for you and your ability.

★ For cruising in retro style, go for a long board or Malibu. These are up to 9-10 feet long and easy to learn on.

★ Shortboards are harder to master but are more manoeuverable once you are up and riding.

★ Mini-mals make a good halfway house. These come in at about 7-8 feet and give you the best of both worlds.

★ Wetsuits are now warmer and more flexible than ever, which means you can surf all year round if you want to.

★ Choose the wetsuit for the season you want to surf in: spring, summer or winter. If you intend to surf all year round, buy the warmest one you can afford.

★ Surf shops, once you get over the cooler-than-you attitude, will help you out with your choices. Don't be afraid of the people who run them. They were learners once too.

LEARNING THE SURFING BASICS

Learning to surf can be a frustrating experience. The sea conditions change all the time and the waves you want aren't always there. Maybe that's why it's got such allure. You spend more time hoping than you actually do surfing.

The best way to learn in the UK is at a British Surfing Association Surf School. It's surprisingly cheap and it will get you surfing faster than if you rented a board for the day and tried to learn on your own. Check out www.britsurf.co.uk

PASSING MUSTER WITH THE SURFING SET

Want to fit in? Then follow a few simple rules and you'll be ok.

- ★ Drop the dude, dude. No one talks like that. Not even us surfers.
- ★ Got all the gear? It usually means no idea. 'Fraid so.
- ★ Be friendly. Surfers, like all decent folk, respond well to friendly people.
- ★ Learn the rules. There is order to the chaos. Understand it and you'll slot right in.
- ★ No one owns the sea. Be respectful but remember that locals don't own the beach.
- ★ Get the right equipment for your ability and the waves you intend to ride. That way you'll improve quicker. Talk to your local surf shop.

A BIT OF SURF SCIENCE

Really? Yes, I am afraid so. You need to understand what the ocean is doing and how waves are created. Once you get a little bit of science under your belt you'll be better able to predict what's going to happen.

Waves are created out at sea by the wind. The stronger the wind blows, and the longer it blows for, the bigger the waves.

Storms far out at sea create the best waves, called ground swells. They have further to travel and the longer they travel, the better they will be. The longer the fetch – the area over which the winds blow – the better the waves.

The best conditions will be when the wind blows offshore (from the shore to the sea). The wind makes the wave faces smooth. Often if there is a ground swell but local onshore winds, you can find a beach that has good waves just by going somewhere where the wind blows offshore.

SURVIVING RIPS AND CURRENTS

Most people get into trouble at the seaside when they get caught in currents. When there is surf or big tidal movements there can be a lot of water rushing in towards the beach. It has to go out again and this creates currents.

You can usually spot currents and rips because the water's surface will be ruffled and more like a river than the sea. Rip currents that head straight out to sea are the most dangerous because it is tempting to swim straight back towards the beach if you get caught in them. It may feel like the obvious thing to do but you'll be swimming forever. The wise move is to swim at right angles to the current until you reach calmer water where there is no current. Then you'll be able to swim in to shore. If you surf, you can use currents to get beyond the breaking waves – but only if you know what you are doing.

NASTIES IN THE WATER

There are sharks in UK coastal waters but you're very unlikely to see them. They live in deep water and don't cruise the beaches looking for weaklings to maul. So when you hear about holidaymakers spotting Great Whites off Cornwall it is (er, probably) just wishful thinking. You might see a basking shark (see our wildlife watching guide on pages 62-65) but, despite their size, they are plankton feeders and non-aggressive.

You're more likely to step on a weaver fish. It is small but has venomous spines which are, apparently, pretty painful. In summer, weaver fish can appear at low tide. If you do get stung, surfing lore dictates that you should wee on it or get a friend to wee on it, because urine will help to neutralise the poison. Does it work? Never tried it. In 25 years of surfing I have never been stung, so I'd say don't fear the water.

WHERE TO SURF

There are some amazing places to surf in the UK. Pretty much anywhere there is a coast with waves, you'll find people taking to the water.

Here's my whistle-stop guide to the best surfing beaches of the UK and Ireland. For more information go online or check out some of the many surf guidebooks on the market. The *Stormrider Guides* are the best.

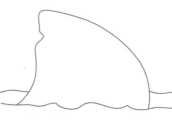

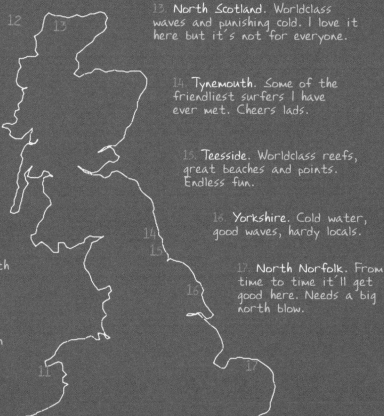

1. Isle of Wight. On its day... classic. Watch out for the Ventnor Vandals.

2. Bournemouth. There is an artificial reef here to make more of the swells that push up the English Channel.

3. Sennen Cove. Beautiful beach, clean water, picks up lots of swell.

4. Gwithian. Popular hot spot near Hayle. Big beach and loads of opportunities.

5. Newquay. Surf city UK with lots of choice of waves for surfers of all abilities. Lots of surf shops.

6. Polzeath. Classic Cornish beach break. Good scene for posh teenagers.

7. Bude area. Good waves for people of all abilities. Home to Big Blue Surf School.

8. Croyde/Saunton/Woolacombe. Nearest quality surf 'to' London. Always busy.

9. The Gower. Swansea's very own surfers' playground.

10. Pembrokeshire. Clean water and beautiful waves. Top camper vanning spot.

11. Hell's Mouth. Home to some good waves and a busy surf scene. Nearest spot to Manchester and Liverpool. Say hello to Dave and Spout.

12. Outer Hebrides. Undiscovered secrets for the explorers among you. Perfect camper van territory.

13. North Scotland. Worldclass waves and punishing cold. I love it here but it's not for everyone.

14. Tynemouth. Some of the friendliest surfers I have ever met. Cheers lads.

15. Teesside. Worldclass reefs, great beaches and points. Endless fun.

16. Yorkshire. Cold water, good waves, hardy locals.

17. North Norfolk. From time to time it'll get good here. Needs a big north blow.

IRELAND

18. The Dingle Peninsula. Home to some cracking waves. And a friendly dolphin. Good for a van trip.

19. Lahinch. Proper men ride mountains here. Beginners stick to the beaches.

20. Donegal Bay and Sligo. Oh my word. Hawaii of the north. Famous the world over.

JUMP RUN KITE SKIM SLIDE FLY CLIMB PADDLE

Of course it isn't all about the surf. There is plenty of other exciting stuff you can get up to. Extreme or adrenaline sports are big news these days. So they should be. Anything that gets your pulse racing and makes you feel like you're really and truly alive is worth doing. Couch potatoes need not apply. Here are just a few ideas:

COASTEERING (West Wales)

Coasteering was invented by the surfers of Pembrokeshire looking for thrills on flat summer days. They started exploring the coast, developed this bonkers pastime and gave it a name. Basically you jump, scramble, climb and swim your way around the coast. What fun! Great team-building exercise for the corporate minded, and fun days out for everyone else. Adventure centres now run coasteering days all around the coast but Pembrokeshire remains the spiritual home. See www.tyf.com for more details.

SKIMBOARDING (south coast, Paignton)

Run, drop, slide. It's not as easy as it looks. The days when we used to slip around on plywood discs are over. Nowadays skimboarding has become a sport in its own right. It's great on long flat beaches but it's even better on steep-shelving sandy beaches with big waves. Once you get the hang of it, you skim out and then surf back. Most of us will perform involuntary acrobatics. Expect a lot of sand in your shorts or bikini. Get more inspiration from www.sandskater.com.

WAKEBOARDING (North Wales, Abersoch)

If you've got a big fast boat and a nice stretch of calm water you could be in for all kinds of towing adventures. Wakeboarding is the daddy. It has gone vertical in recent times. Don't expect David Niven cruising around the bay; expect slides, shove-its and ollies. If you're new to it, expect a few faceplants too. Lots of estuaries, lakes, rivers and stretches of open water are perfect. For the best action check out Wakestock in North Wales at www.wakestock.co.uk.

CANOEING (Canolfan Tryweryn, National Whitewater Centre)

It's been a long time since I sat in a canoe. Things have moved on since then, thankfully. Nowadays you can take to the water in all kinds of craft, just about anywhere you fancy. From Canadian canoes to whitewater mayhem – it's all out there. Start on the flat stuff and work your way up from there. The National Whitewater Centre in North Wales can give you all the training you need – see www.ukrafting.co.uk.

CLIMBING (Cairngorms, Scotland, Peak District, Lake District)

You'll need mountains or cliffs to do this and your camper is the perfect vehicle to take you there. I'm no good with heights so I am always impressed by those who aren't afraid to throw themselves upon the mercy of the rock. You need to be strong, agile and fearless to get the most out of it. A great way to get going, so they tell me, is to go to an indoor climbing wall. Once you've learned the ropes (literally), fire up the combi and head for the hills. Just make sure you know what you're doing and are aware of the risks. Start with www.thebmc.co.uk.

KITE SURFING (Tiree, Scotland, Brandon Bay, Ireland)

This looks hard. A big kite and a small board? I've never tried to do this but plenty of people have. You can kite surf on pretty much any stretch of water anywhere. You don't even need waves, so it's perfect for the more sheltered locations with plenty of wind but not much in the way of surf. Find out more by getting in touch with the British Kite Surfing Association – see www.britishkitesurfingassociation.co.uk for locations, training and events. The experts head to Tiree for the UK's best conditions and Brandon Bay for Ireland's finest.

KITE BUGGYING AND BOARDING (Westward Ho! Devon)

Basically the same as kite surfing but with wheels on. Sort of. Having never tried it I can only assume – from a safe distance – that it hurts more when you get it wrong. All it takes is a big gust of wind and you're into the ice cream van. But of course it's not like that at all once you've learned properly and know what you're doing. Lots of local clubs will show you how. Respect to the guys and girls who master it. Westward Ho! is fast becoming a fave location.

WHITTLING THE TIME AWAY

Maybe dangerous sports aren't your thing. Or perhaps you had a little too much mojo in your mojito last night. Fair enough. Put the kettle on and do something altogether less demanding. After all, it is Sunday morning and you're camping. It's an idler's paradise.

Here are a few ideas for ways to waste your time brilliantly:

MAKE YOUR VERY OWN ANDY GOLDSWORTHY

Andy Goldsworthy is considered by many to be the father of 'rock balancing', an activity that seems to be growing more and more popular among people with far too much time on their hands.

I am sure he'll rue the day he ever balanced one stone on top of the other, with philistines like me suggesting mindless cairn-building around the countryside, but it makes a point about what this great environmental artist has achieved. It's natural, it's healthy, it's fun, it's not as easy as it looks and everyone loves to do it. Imitation is the sincerest form of flattery. We love beautiful objects and a pile of stones photographed against a landscape can be very special indeed.

Find three flat, round rocks. Put the largest on the ground. Balance the middle one on top and then the smallest on top of that. You now have yourself your very own 'Andy Goldsworthy' (style) sculpture.

How high can you go?

MAKE A DRIFTWOOD SUN SHADE

On some beaches there is so much driftwood that you could go into business making picture frames for the tourists. On others you'd be lucky to find enough to whittle. So, if you find yourself on a beach with plenty of it, why not give yourself a task and build a driftwood sun shade? It's easy. All you need is five long and relatively straight pieces of driftwood and a bunch of other shorter pieces. You could opt to use something like bracken or long grass for the shade, or go for more driftwood – it's up to you.

Begin by finding two uprights of the same length (about 1-1.25 meters or 3-4 feet long) plus another piece of about the same length to be a cross bar. Lash the pieces together with old fishing net or rope you find on the beach or, better still, some long grass.

Bury the uprights in the sand or pebbles and make sure they are facing the right way to provide you with shade.

Use the two longest pieces to make two rear supports for the frame. This should create a goalpost with two rear sloping supports, which will form the roof frame.

Place the shorter pieces of wood across the sloping rear supports to provide a structure for the roofing materials to rest upon. Lash them on with rope or fishing twine.

Cover the roof with bracken, grass or anything else you can find. Tarpaulins, tablecloths and sheets are quite acceptable but just remember to take them home again after you've had your day on the beach. You could even just use driftwood like this one here. It provides a nice dappled shade. If you've used all natural materials then leave it for someone else to enjoy. Nature will take care of the rest.

217

WHITTLING STICKS

If you've remembered your Swiss Army knife and a deckchair and have a whole morning ahead of you, but don't fancy going on a long walk or hiking up a mountain, then whittling could be just the thing. It'll prepare you for more rigorous adventures ahead (if you decide to make a wizard's staff) and gives you a jolly good excuse for doing virtually nothing at all. Master whittling and you've earned yourself a PhD from the university of looking busy doing nothing much at all.

Working in wood is, needless to say, very satisfying. Even now, after all these years of evolution and Xboxes, we still need to find things for idle thumbs to do. Start with something simple like a walking stick. With a sharp blade you can score the bark and make pretty patterns. Find a nicely gnarly length and you could fashion something altogether more elaborate. Perhaps a 'priest' for dispatching fish, arrows for your home-made bow or a rustic key ring. Before you know it we'll have you selling carved wooden mushrooms at the side of the road. Or maybe not.

MAKE A ROPE SWING IN THE WOODS

If you ever find a bit of rope lying about, don't forget to pack it into a corner of your van. It can be useful for all sorts of things. One of those is a rope swing. All you really need is a tree with an overhanging branch, a piece of rope and a couple of hours to waste.

The best swings are those on sloping ground or over a river. It adds a bit of danger. As you push yourself off, the ground will drop away from beneath you and make you feel like you're swinging over an abyss. The best swing we ever made was out of a buoy we found on the beach. We took it up to the woods and swung on it all afternoon. Such fun.

SUNDAY LUNCH

A time for family
and friends

Even if you're in the back of beyond, Sunday lunch should still be special. It's a time for sitting around a big table with family and friends, catching up on the week's events, eating a beautifully cooked meal and generally making a bit of an effort. So why not now, out in the wilds?

YOUR SUNDAY BEST

You might not be able to cook a full roast dinner but there are plenty of things you can do that are equally splendid. If you've got a Dutch oven you could try an amazing beef pot roast (see pages 140-141). You could stoke up the barbie and enjoy a juicy steak and salad. Or you could try our delicious Sunday best-ever recipes.

Whatever you decide, Sunday lunch is a special time. Get out the bunting, plonk the plonk to cool in the river, invite the nearest neighbours round and put on your own Sunday gathering. And don't forget your Sunday best. Best-ever, that is.

PICK-YOUR-OWN

For those who find foraging a step too far, pick-your-own provides a great halfway house. In late spring and summer, you can get your hands on all kinds of fabulous field-fresh produce. There's a lot more to it than strawberries: raspberries, black-currants, gooseberries, redcurrants, peas, broad beans – you name it, you can have it. Some farms, like our own local PYO, Ashford Inn in North Devon, have tabletop picking with the strawberries at shoulder height so you don't even have to bend down to pick them. They are so sweet and delicious that it's hard to go home with only one punnet.

Like many clever ideas, pick-your-own is beneficial to everyone involved. For the growers it means they don't necessarily have to get involved with the big supermarkets, gives them top dollar for their produce and saves them the job of harvesting and packaging. It's a win-win situation, so to speak. I imagine that most people will get so seduced by the experience, like us, that they will pick far more than they need. That's when you learn how to make jam.

As a style of shopping, it's also got advantages over going to the supermarket: the produce is as fresh as fresh can be, you know where it comes from, there's precious little packaging, your food miles are minimal and you are benefiting the local community by giving your money directly to the farmer. And what about the experience? Picking strawberries to the sound of birdsong on a summer's day is another one of those special days out. What's not to love?

Just make sure you've got some clotted cream, Greek yoghurt or chocolate in the van. Afterwards you'll be able to park up somewhere quiet and scoff the lot.

CHOCOLATE strawberries

→ This is another favourite. Our kids love it, so for once we don't mind them going choco-crazy – at least they are getting fruit at the same time.

Break up a bar of milk or plain chocolate into a mug, then place the mug into a pan of hot water. This will create a primitive bain-marie, which is a good way of transferring gentle heat to the chocolate so that it doesn't burn. Make sure the chocolate doesn't come into direct contact with the water. When your chocolate has melted to perfection, hold your strawberries by the stalk, and dip them to cover them in chocolate. Place them on a cool plate and put in the fridge to chill. In twenty minutes or so the chocolate should be hard and ready to eat. Yum!

STRAWBERRIES and CREAM

→ I know you don't need any help with this but I thought it might be good to pass on a little trick of ours to make clotted cream taste even better than it does already. Dollop a few large tablespoons of clotted cream into a bowl and add five or six drops of vanilla extract. Give it a stir and then spoon on to a bowl of freshly picked strawberries with a sprinkling of caster sugar. It's the taste of an English summer. And a little bit naughty too, especially if you're watching the weight.

Pick-your-own bowl of SUMMER

✳ Whichever berries you've been picking, and whether from the hedgerows or a local farm, eat them as fresh as you can and enjoy them simply.

Blackberries always seem to taste best when just picked while strolling along a country lane but are also delicious stirred into a bowl of lightly cooked and sweetened warm apple.

Try hulled and halved strawberries sprinkled with sugar and a touch of good balsamic vinegar – you might like to get really adventurous and add a sprinkle of black pepper too. Strawberries are also delicious sprinkled with sugar and a little lemon zest and maybe some shredded basil.

Raspberries, tayberries and loganberries like a sprinkling of orange zest, sugar and a little finely shredded mint. Toss with redcurrants and ripe stoned and halved cherries too for a bowl of beauty.

Crème fraiche, double cream and Greek yoghurt are all perfect partners, as is a sprinkle of meringue added along the way. You might like to try a drizzle of honey and a spoonful of Greek yoghurt too with the fruits of your labour for breakfast.

PICK-YOUR-OWNS

SHARCOTT FARM, EXMOOR

The moor's first pick-your-own blueberry farm opened its doors in 2009. The season lasts from August until September so there's only a short window to pick your own bucket of this wonderful superfood. And they are kind to bumblebees. If you can, go!

www.exmoorblueberries.co.uk

COPAS FARMS, BUCKS

Best farms in the region, with over 1500 acres. That's what they say. And why not? With two farms at Cookham and Iver in Bucks it's a pick-your-own heaven. Delicious fruit and vegetables all through the growing season. Bloomin' lovely, according to Cath.

www.copasfarms.co.uk

TIPTREE FARM, ESSEX

Worth a look, says Sarah. She's been there a few times and loves it. It is one of the oldest pick-your-owns, and is a great supporter of heritage fruit varieties. Tiptree also do their own jams and pickles.

www.tiptree.com

VALE OF CAMELOT GROWERS, SOMERSET

Open to the public for hanging baskets and plants around mid-May, then open for the pick-your-own fruit season with strawberries and gooseberries, then raspberries in July. It's all grown naturally, out in the open without a polytunnel in sight.

Tel: 01963 440280

WIVETON HALL, NORTH NORFOLK

Go here for the soft fruits, asparagus and artichokes, or just for the wonderful café that brings in walkers from the coast path as well as fruit pickers. Don't miss the delicious scones and strawberry jam for tea.

www.wivetonhall.co.uk

COOK'S YARD FARM, EAST SUSSEX

Here's a novel idea that actually makes picking your own into 'picking your own'.
Rent a cherry tree and then come and pick from your own tree to enjoy the fruits
of your (someone else's) labour before the birdies get them. In 2009 the average
renter picked 15 kilos of cherries. That's a lot of pies. Great stuff.

www.rentacherrytree.co.uk

TULLY'S FARM, WEST SUSSEX

There's a lot more to it than just picking your own, although that's pretty good.
You can even play Farmer's Golf, which sounds a bit mad. In the summer get lost
in the Maize maze.

www.tullysfarm.com

PETERLEY MANOR FARM, BUCKS

Another fine pick-your-own with a great farm shop and nursery and plenty of
fresh seasonal veg. You can even get your Christmas tree here (although I think
they pick them for you).

www.peterleymanorfarm.co.uk

KENYON HALL FARM, WARRINGTON, CHESHIRE

Visit during early summer and you'll be rewarded with fresh English asparagus.
You also find plenty of summer fruits and veg throughout the season and can even
pick up your Hallowe'en squashes and pumpkins come October. Woooooooo!

www.kenyonhall.co.uk

If none of these is anywhere near you, look online at www.pickyourown.info
for a handy map and list of farms.

FUN FOR THE LITTLE NIPPERS
TIME TO GO CRABBING

Got a little time to spare at high tide? Go crabbing. It is a serious business – and serious fun. At worst it'll give you an hour or so perched on a rock by the water's edge or on a quayside, looking down at the milky water, waiting patiently for a bite. It's not a bad way to take a little time out, is it? I know some people who could use a few hours like that. Crabbing can turn a dull afternoon by the water into a couple of exciting hours of laughter, screaming and toe-pinching fun that's as traditional as fish and chips and a lot better for you.

I wouldn't count on crabbing for a meal though. It's strictly for entertainment. You are very, very unlikely to catch an edible crab that's big enough for the pot. Having said that, if it's brown and more than 14 centimetres across its shell, it's definitely a keeper. Lucky you!

For successful crabbing you don't have to use traditional crab lines with nasty little hooks. You won't even have to spend hours trying to prise a few innocent limpets off the rocks for bait either. These days crabbing is cruelty-free and it's all the better for it – although vegetarians might disagree – because the wonder-bait of the moment is uncooked, slightly 'off' bacon. If you're a fan of a proper camper van breakfast there will be some already festering in the icebox. Crabs will love it.

MAKING YOUR OWN CRAB LINE

A day spent crabbing can be very cheap entertainment. All it will cost you is the price of a pack of bacon, especially if you make your own lines. You will need about ten metres of string or fishing line, a plastic bottle, one of those nylon string bags you put your washing tablets in and a weight of some kind. A pebble will do, as long as it's heavy enough to sink the bag to the bottom. Tie the bag to the end of the string, put your weight in the bag, then tie the other end of the string around the bottle. Wind up the string around the bottle and you're ready to go. Your bait, the bacon, goes straight into the bag. Just cut it up into little pieces first. Now for the important bit. Find a quayside or rock pool where there is a good depth of water.

High tide or a rising tide will usually be best. Sling your bag into the water and let out the line until it touches the bottom. Then wait.

You can catch crabs with washing tablet bags because crabs go for the bait and get their claws tangled up in the bag. When you lift it up out of the water after a few minutes, the greedy little crustaceans will hang on long enough for you to haul them out into your bucket. Or not.

This method is pretty effective and will sometimes allow you to haul two or more crabs out in one go. The best thing is that it won't hurt the crabs so, once you've had enough, you can just tip them back into the water – ready for the next crabber to throw his line in.

CRAB CARE

Crabbing is fun and should be as cruelty-free as possible. You're not going to eat them so treat them as well as you can. If you aren't going to throw them back straight away, store them in a bucket with plenty of fresh salt water. Don't over-crowd them either. They might get stressed. You don't want to upset a crab. They have claws.

PLACES TO GO CRABBING

You could probably catch a crab from almost any saltwater quayside, anywhere in the UK. Muddy bottoms can help, which is why a lot of the better locations are on estuaries. But try it anywhere – a quayside, from the rocks, in rock pools. Just be aware of the tides and don't allow yourself to get cut off. Always make sure you can see your pathway back to safety.

High tide or a rising tide is rumoured to be best for crabbing because the little blighters come out to get the good stuff that comes in as the sea rises around them.

COMPETITION CRABBING

At certain times of the year, on quaysides all across the UK, amateur crabbers jostle for best position in a series of crabbing competitions. Rules differ wherever you go. There are prizes for catching the most.

Here are just a few competitions to look out for:

★ Walberswick, Norfolk. British Open Championship is held here in July so it must be good.

★ Appledore, North Devon. A lovely village with a perfect crabbing quayside (high tide only). Open competition in August.

★ Herne Bay, Kent. Competition from Herne Bay Pier during the Herne Bay Festival.

★ Wivenhoe, Essex. Competition on the quayside in September.

★ Flushing, Cornwall. Competitions often take place during Flushing Regatta.

★ Swanage, Dorset. Annual Swanage Carnival has sideshow crabbing competitions.

EXPECT TO SEE LOTS OF...

Shore crabs. These green or brown crabs are very common. As 'peelers' (when they shed their hard shells and are soft and vulnerable) they are very useful as bait. Bass, apparently, will fall over each other to nab them. Although not the ones I use.

Blue velvet swimmer crabs. They have thick soft hairs on their legs and bodies. Underneath, blueish shells and mad-looking red eyes. They measure on average about 8cm across the shell. In the UK we don't tend to eat them but they are edible.

BUT NOT SO MANY...

Spider crabs. These tend to live a little further out for most of the year, but in summer they come in closer to shore to mate (they think) – this is when you might be lucky and catch one on your washing bag. If you do, and it's big enough, take it home and cook it up. They are delicious.

Brown crabs. These are the ones that look like pies and the ones that you'll see on saucy postcards nipping the vicar's toes. They can be big. Very edible, but make sure they measure over 14cm across the shell.

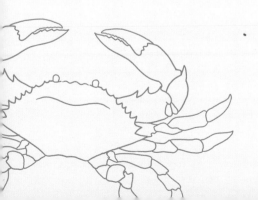

GRIDDLED HALLOUMI with crushed peas, MINT and ROCKET

If you haven't gorged yourself on the pick-your-own in the morning, then you're going to need a decent starter for Sunday lunch. This recipe is fresh, minty and just perfect for amusing your *bouche* before the main event. Maggie and Charlie love halloumi (or squeaky cheese as it's known) because it's about as much fun as cheese gets (yes, better than a fondue).

Halloumi can be cooked under the grill, on the barbecue or on a griddle. If you've never tried it, try it today.

FOR 4 AS A STARTER

6 HANDFULS COOKED FRESH OR FROZEN PEAS, DRAINED
3 TBSP FINELY SLICED MINT
1 LEMON, HALVED
OLIVE OIL
4-6 SLICES HALLOUMI (ABOUT 250G)
4 HANDFULS ROCKET LEAVES

Preheat a griddle. Tip the peas into a pan and mash them with a potato masher (or back of a fork) so they are slightly crushed. Heat them gently. As you do so, mix the mint and 2 generous squirts of lemon juice into the peas and season. Drizzle the griddle with olive oil and griddle the halloumi over a high heat for 1-2 minutes on each side, or until slightly charred.

Toss the rocket with a little olive oil, a touch of lemon juice and some seasoning. Put a handful of dressed rocket on each plate (or pile everything on a platter). Next, add a heap of the minty peas to each plate and top with the hot halloumi. Scatter any leftover rocket leaves on top. Slice the other lemon half into four wedges and put one on each plate.

Asparagus 3 WAYS

Asparagus is a great one to cook in season, which in the UK is May and June. When the time comes, nip out and gorge yourselves.

FOR 4 AS A STARTER
24 ASPARAGUS SPEARS

Trim away any tough parts of the stems before steaming or simmering the asparagus in boiling water for 3-4 minutes or until just tender (or cooking it on the barbecue). Drain and serve hot or cold, dressed with one of the following finishing flourishes:

SOY, HONEY and Sesame

2 TBSP DARK SOY SAUCE
2 TBSP RUNNY HONEY
1 TBSP SESAME SEEDS
SQUEEZE OF LEMON (OR LIME) JUICE

Return the cooked asparagus to the pan with the soy, honey, sesame seeds and lemon juice and heat for a minute or so, swirling the juices around. Tip into shallow bowls to eat with bread.

Chilli, LEMON and olive oil

JUICE OF 1 SMALL LEMON
½-1 RED CHILLI, DESEEDED AND FINELY CHOPPED
2 TBSP OLIVE OIL

Mix the ingredients together in a small bowl. Arrange the cooked asparagus on a platter or plate, spoon over the dressing and sprinkle with sea salt.

Crispy BACON and ALMONDS

4 RASHERS STREAKY BACON, CHOPPED SMALL

2 TBSP CHOPPED ALMONDS (OR PINE NUTS OR HAZELNUTS)

4 TBSP OLIVE OIL

2 GENEROUS PINCHES OF SMOKED PAPRIKA (OPTIONAL)

Fry the bacon in a pan until really crisp, adding the almonds halfway through. Leave to cool completely so the nuts crisp up. Mix the oil with the smoked paprika, if using. Arrange the cooked asparagus on a platter or plate. Scatter the bacon and nuts over the top and drizzle with the olive oil. Eat as soon as possible.

Everyone loves a tasty bit of finger food. Something to amuse your taste buds before the main event. Go for it with slices of griddled pitta, radishes, celery, cucumber, cooked new potatoes, baby carrots, chunks of fennel, crisps or elegant grissini.

CAMPER van chunky houmous with PINE NUTS

This might not be absolutely authentic but it's still really tasty. If you can't get the ingredients where you're camping, just cheat! Buy a pot of ready made houmous and top with a drizzle of good olive oil and a scattering of toasted pine nuts.

FOR 6-8

1 X 400G TIN CHICKPEAS, DRAINED AND RINSED

1 CLOVE GARLIC, CRUSHED

JUICE OF HALF A LEMON (OR MAYBE A LITTLE MORE)

1 TSP GROUND CUMIN

GENEROUS PINCH OF CRUSHED DRIED CHILLIES

4 TBSP OLIVE OIL, PLUS EXTRA TO DRIZZLE

3 TBSP TAHINI PASTE

1 TBSP PINE NUTS

Tip the chickpeas into a bowl and add the garlic, lemon juice, spices, 4 tablespoons of oil, the tahini paste and half a teaspoon of salt. Stir all the ingredients together, then mash to a thick-textured creamy purée using a potato masher. You will need to mash for a good 5 minutes or so and even then the houmous will still have chunky pieces of chickpea in it but that is its charm.

Add a tablespoon of cold water to thin the houmous and give it a good mix, adding a little more water if you think it needs it. Taste to check the seasoning: you may want to add a touch more salt or lemon juice, as houmous needs plenty of seasoning to bring out the flavours.

To finish, toast the pine nuts in a frying pan until golden – for about a minute, giving them a shake now and then. Serve the houmous drizzled with a little extra oil and scattered with the pine nuts.

Spiced yoghurt, SPINACH and SULTANA dip

FOR 4-6

8 TBSP NATURAL YOGHURT

1 CLOVE GARLIC, CRUSHED

1 TSP MEDIUM CURRY PASTE

2 TBSP SHREDDED OR CHOPPED YOUNG LEAF SPINACH

1 TSP CHOPPED MINT (OPTIONAL)

1 TBSP SULTANAS

In a bowl, mix the yoghurt, garlic and curry paste with a pinch of salt. Stir in the spinach, mint (if using) and sultanas.

Hasta la salsa

Don't make this too far ahead as it will go watery. The other option is to cheat and buy a pot of ready made salsa and stir chilli, coriander and lime into it.

FOR 4-6

3 RIPE TOMATOES, CHOPPED SMALL

½ RED CHILLI, DESEEDED AND FINELY CHOPPED

2-3 TBSP CHOPPED CORIANDER LEAVES

ZEST AND JUICE OF 1 LIME

1 TSP SUGAR

Mix everything together in a bowl with a pinch of salt and leave aside for 15 minutes or so before eating to let the flavours mingle.

The boyfriend POTATO SALAD

Once upon a time, in the days before I came along, Joanne went off on a camping and hostelling trip around California. This recipe is something she picked up along the way. An all-American boy called Brad taught her how to make it, which is why it's known as the boyfriend salad in our house. It's simple and easy and it has that laid back, sunny-all-year-round California style about it. Just like Brad. Not that I'm jealous or anything.

You can also add lardons or bacon to this to give it an extra smoky flavour. It's great as an accompaniment to barbecued meat and a green salad.

FOR 4

 GENEROUS DOUBLE HANDFUL SMALLISH NEW POTATOES

4 MEDIUM OR LARGE FRESH FREE-RANGE EGGS

2-3 TBSP CRÈME FRAICHE

3 SPRING ONIONS, FINELY CHOPPED

1 TBSP CHOPPED DILL (OPTIONAL)

Halve or quarter the potatoes, depending on size, then simmer them in salted water for about 10 minutes or until tender. Drain and allow to cool off for a few minutes.

Meanwhile bring another pan of water to the boil and hard-boil the eggs for about 7-8 minutes. They can still have slightly soft centres but you don't want them to be runny.

Cool the eggs in a bowl of water and then peel and quarter them. In a large bowl mix all the ingredients and season. Serve while everything is still slightly warm.

ONE-PAN chicken (or rabbit) with TARRAGON, lemon & garlic

If you're eating outside and barbecuing your starter, you can get this dish done ahead in the van and keep it warm in a tin over the embers while you're eating your starter. This is a really fresh and zesty dish to have with your forager's salad (see page 259) or, if you haven't the time to go searching for foliage, serve it with a leafy green salad instead. Rabbit will give it a gamey touch if you fancy it.

FOR 4

OLIVE OIL

KNOB OF BUTTER, PLUS 1 TBSP

8 SHALLOTS (HALVED IF LARGE)

4 CHICKEN LEGS OR RABBIT PORTIONS

2 SMALL WINE GLASSFULS OF WHITE WINE

300ML CHICKEN STOCK

12 CHERRY TOMATOES, HALVED

3 TBSP CHOPPED TARRAGON

2 CLOVES GARLIC, FINELY CHOPPED

FINELY GRATED ZEST OF 1 LEMON

Heat a generous splash of oil and the knob of butter together in a large, shallow-sided pan. Over a high heat, brown the shallots in the hot fat, then scoop them out of the pan and on to a plate. Brown the chicken or rabbit in a single layer (do this in two batches if your pan isn't big enough) until it is a deep golden colour on both sides, adding a little more oil and butter if necessary. Return the shallots to the pan to join the chicken or rabbit.

Next add the wine and boil to reduce by half. Pour in the stock and bring to the boil. Reduce the heat to medium and dot the tablespoon of butter into the liquid and add some seasoning. Leave the chicken or rabbit to bubble away, submerged in the liquid and uncovered, for 20-25 minutes – the idea is that the liquid reduces as the meat cooks. Five minutes before the end of the cooking time, add the cherry tomatoes and tarragon to the pan. Taste and add more seasoning if needed.

Mix the garlic with the lemon zest. Take the pan off the heat, sprinkle the garlicky lemon zest over the chicken and tuck in.

Griddled vegetables with MOZZARELLA, chickpeas and plenty of HERBS

A meal in itself. If you want to fire up the barbie you can do the vegetables that way too – barbecued halloumi is a good alternative to the mozzarella. Eat warm or at room temperature. Without the mozzarella it also makes a good side dish to serve 6, to accompany sausages or griddled meats or fish.

FOR 4

4 COURGETTES

1 LARGE AUBERGINE

2 RED PEPPERS

3 TBSP CHOPPED MINT

4 TBSP TORN BASIL

4 TBSP OLIVE OIL, PLUS EXTRA FOR GRIDDLING AND DRIZZLING

1 FAT CLOVE GARLIC, CRUSHED

1 X 410G TIN CHICKPEAS, DRAINED

CRUSHED DRIED CHILLIES, TO SPRINKLE

2 BALLS (EACH 125G) MOZZARELLA

Trim and slice the courgettes and aubergines lengthways – you should get 4 or 5 slices from the courgettes and 8-10 from the aubergine. Deseed and slice the peppers into strips. Preheat a griddle.

Mix the herbs in a medium-sized bowl with the 4 tablespoons of olive oil and the garlic, chickpeas and a generous pinch or two of crushed sea salt.

Brush the griddle with oil and griddle the vegetables for 2-3 minutes on each side until charred and tender. As they are ready, put them on to a plate.

Spoon half the chickpeas on to a platter. Layer the griddled courgettes, aubergine and peppers on top in a pile (time to get artistic), adding a drizzle of olive oil and a sprinkling of sea salt and crushed dried chillies as you go (the chillies can be quite fiery so proceed with caution – you can always add more as you eat). Scatter the remaining herby chickpeas around the vegetables.

Slice or tear the mozzarella and arrange on top of the vegetables. Add a final drizzle of olive oil and a sprinkle of chilli.

SAUSAGES with beans, TOMATOES and ROSEMARY

This is a hearty bean and sausage stew for a crisp autumn day when there's the beginning of a nip in the air. It'll warm those tootsies right up. This could be a meal in itself but would be equally good with something green on the side – a salad or fresh green veg. And perhaps some toasted French bread, rubbed with a little garlic. This also works well using a tin of cooked green lentils instead of beans.

FOR 4

OIL

8 PLUMP HERBY PORK SAUSAGES

2 TBSP BUTTER

3 ONIONS, PEELED AND FINELY SLICED

2 CLOVES GARLIC, FINELY SLICED

2 TBSP FINELY CHOPPED FRESH ROSEMARY

1 TSP SUGAR

1 X 410G TIN CANNELLINI OR BUTTER BEANS, DRAINED

1 X 400G TIN CHOPPED TOMATOES

2 TBSP TOMATO PURÉE (NOT ESSENTIAL)

250ML CHICKEN OR BEEF STOCK

1 HEAPED TBSP GRAINY MUSTARD

Heat a splash of oil in a medium to large, shallow-sided pan. Brown the sausages in the oil until golden all over, then scoop them out of the pan and on to a plate.

Add the butter to the pan and, when melted, tip in the onions, garlic, rosemary, sugar and seasoning. Cook over a medium heat, uncovered, for 15 minutes or until the onions are golden and soft – give them a stir from time to time.

Next stir in the beans, tomatoes, tomato purée, stock and mustard and nestle the sausages back in amongst everything. Bring to the boil, then reduce the heat to medium, cover and simmer gently for 15 minutes. Taste to check the seasoning before ladling into bowls.

Summer PUDDINGS

Red- and blackcurrants give summer puddings an intense fruity flavour but black-berries, blueberries, loganberries and cherries also work well in the mix. Finish off with a few extra berries if you are feeling fancy.

FOR 4

1/4 MUGFUL (ABOUT 75G) DE-STALKED REDCURRANTS

1/4 MUGFUL (ABOUT 75G) DE-STALKED BLACKCURRANTS

1 1/2 MUGFULS (ABOUT 200G) RASPBERRIES

3 TBSP SUGAR

1 TSP MINT, FINELY CHOPPED

4 THINNISH SLICES WHITE BREAD

WHIPPED OR CLOTTED CREAM

Tip the prepared fruit into a medium-sized pan with the sugar and four table-spoons of water. Give everything a mix and bring to simmering point, stirring to dissolve the sugar. Reduce the heat, partially cover and gently simmer the fruit for 2-3 minutes so the juices run. Keep an eye on the fruit as it simmers and don't overcook it – you want to keep the fresh flavour and the whole texture of the ber-ries. Stir in the mint and leave to cool slightly.

Cut the crusts off the bread. Cut each slice of bread into 3 fingers and then cut each finger in half. Put a few pieces of bread in to the bottom of four smallish tumbler-style glasses (or cups) and spoon two tablespoons of the juicy cooked fruit in to each one. Add another layer of bread to each and then divide the remaining fruit and juice between the glasses. You want the bread to be soaked in the juices and the flavours to mix, so leave the puddings to cool, then chill well – ideally for several hours. To serve, top each one with a blob of whipped or clotted cream.

Easy FRUITY crumble

I love a crumble so imagine how pleased I was when Sarah suggested this. Crumble in a camper? Without an oven? Great idea!

These are also delicious made with damsons, mixed with a few bilberries or elderberries (but add lots more sugar), blackberry and apple, or apricots or peaches in the summer. To double cheat, sprinkle the fruit with granola (see page 19) instead of making the topping. All you need to eat with these is a spoonful of thick yoghurt or some warm custard if there is a chill in the air.

THIS WILL DO FOR 2 PUDDING LOVERS (OR 4 IF MADE IN SMALL CUPS)

6 VICTORIA OR OTHER PLUMS (ABOUT 300G), STONED AND QUARTERED

ZEST AND JUICE OF HALF AN ORANGE

2 TBSP SUGAR

FOR THE CRUMBLE TOPPING

1 TBSP BUTTER

1 TBSP SUGAR

4 TBSP PORRIDGE OATS

TO FINISH

GREEK YOGHURT OR CUSTARD (OPTIONAL)

Put the plums, orange zest and juice and the sugar into a medium pan. Bring to the boil, then reduce the heat and simmer gently for 8-10 minutes or until soft. Spoon the hot fruit into the bottom of two generous-sized cups or 4 small ones (there may be a little excess juice, in which case… cook's perk). Wash and dry the pan (or use a frying pan for the next stage).

To make the topping, melt the butter in the pan and, when sizzling, tip in the sugar and oats. Toast over the heat, stirring now and then, for 5-7 minutes, then tip into a bowl to cool for 2-3 minutes and to crisp slightly. Sprinkle the crumble topping on to the fruit and eat straight away.

wonderful stuff!

SUNDAY TEA

Hazy Days and
lazy ways

Sunday teatime, another important weekend milestone. Deckchairs are the order of the hour. This is the time for kids to make and fly kites, and for everyone else to kick back. It is customary, at this point, for dads to ignore every bit of chaos from behind the paper. I have a friend, a very seasoned camper van camper, who does this better than anyone I know. There could be absolute carnage going on all around him yet nothing will disturb the ceremonial reading of the cricket or rugby scores.

SQUEEZING EVERY LAST DROP

Why should he care? Everyone is happy. The weekend has a few joys yet to savour. It's time to let the kettle whistle for one last time and take a leisurely walk in the woods before packing up and making ready for the journey home.

For me, someone who can never sit still, Sunday afternoon is a time for twitching. Let's make a dam, play poohsticks, beat the world at conkers! I think it's to do with refusing to believe the weekend is almost done. Once high tea is finished it's time to hit the highway. I am afraid that slightly empty feeling that comes after a great weekend will strike me at any moment. The feeling of going back to work, of Monday morning, of comedown.

But then... I've been a bit peaky, haven't I? The van needs time to rest. No point in thrashing it. I haven't even checked the oil and I have a hammock to make. There are fish to be caught. Blackberries to pick. What's so important about work?

Let's stay another day

BUT FIRST LET'S GO FLY A KITE

What better for a Sunday afternoon adventure than to make a kite? This is the way my granddad taught me to make them. He used to have lots of them that he'd made when he was a boy. Some were six or eight feet across. That was what he was like, always pushing to see just how big or far or fast he could go, which wasn't very fast by modern standards. He was born in 1901.

This kite looks like a proper traditional-style kite, complete with ribbon tail and a single string. It won't do tricks or loop the loop and you can't tow a surfboard behind it. It's a Sunday afternoon kite for flying on Sunday afternoons.

To make your own, all you need is an old piece of sheet, a ball of garden twine, two pieces of bamboo, each about 60cm (2 feet) long (although you really can go as big as you want), and a needle and thread.

HERE'S HOW YOU DO IT

Take the two pieces of bamboo. Cut a notch in each end of both pieces.

Tie them together with a length of twine to make the form of a cross (or a lower case letter 't'). Take care to wrap the twine around the join tightly, so that the joint is sturdy and self-supporting.

Next, wrap one strand of twine around the cross through the notches you made, so that you form a frame. Again, tie it tightly. This is what will support your sheet.

Lay your cross on to the sheet and cut around the string frame, leaving 5cm (2 inches) overlap all the way around.

Sew the sheet on to the string as tightly as you can. Your kite should now start to look like a kite.

Using the spare bits of sheet, cut six strips each about 5cm (2 inches) wide and about 15cm (6 inches) long. Tie them to a piece of string at 30cm (1 foot) intervals. This is the tail of your kite. Tie the tail on to the end of the longest piece of bamboo.

Tie the rest of your string on to the centre point of the cross.

Paint a scary face on to your kite (optional). Now you're ready to go.

To fly your kite you're going to need a windy day and you will probably have to do a bit of running. The person who is going to fly the kite should unwind about 6 metres (20 feet) of twine while another person holds the kite up. The flyer then has to run into the wind as the other person releases the kite. With any luck the kite will rise into the sky, at which point you'll be able to release more and more twine. If not, you'll have to try again.

A WALK IN THE WOODS

When I was a kid I spent so much time in the woods it was ridiculous. I'd rush out as soon as I got home from school and get back just after dark, grubby, tired, hungry and often in trouble. We did all sorts – digging tunnels, making dens, building bike jumps, searching for bones and old bottles. But then it was the seventies and we didn't have much else to do. We hadn't discovered girls or music at that age either.

I've remembered all sorts of things that are still nice to know. If my kids get stung with a stinging nettle then I can show them what they need to make it better. It's hardly survival in the wild but it's still a real pleasure to teach them a few bits of useful woodlore before it gets lost altogether.

★ On nettle stings use dock leaves. They often grow together. It's a yin and yang thing.

★ Sucking the flowers of the white dead-nettle gives you a gorgeous sweet hit of nectar.

★ Moss and lichen generally only grow on the north side of trees. Knowing this can help if you are lost.

★ You can wash your hands with soapwort (the clue is in the name) and a little water.

★ Hazel that has been coppiced (cut back) grows really straight. It has long been used for walking sticks, but is also great for making your own arrows and spears.

★ Yew (preferably dry, not green) is the best wood for making bows.

★ The hairy seeds in rosehips make great itching powder.

★ You can make very basic but really tasty bread over a campfire with just flour and water and a stick.

★ You can't smoke dried cow parsley, no matter what you stuff its hollow centre with.

★ If you squash elderberries on your crisp white school shirt it will look just like fake blood and your mum will think you've been shot. She may get very cross though (probably about getting the elderberry stains out in the wash).

★ You can eat young dandelion leaves but they may have a diuretic effect, hence the French name, pissenlit.

★ If you use a dandelion clock to tell the time you will be late. Blow on it until the seeds have all dispersed. The number of blows it takes is the time.

★ Soft rush, a long dark green grass that grows in clumps in boggy places, can be used to make primitive rope. Just flatten it, split it and plait it. Perfect for constructing a den.

★ Hours can be wasted looking for a four-leaved clover. Lie on your tummy in the grass and examine every one. If you get peckish you can eat the clover leaves.

★ 'Cheesers', horse chestnuts with a flat surface that have grown as one of a pair, are better for playing conkers with than the round ones. Big ones are highly prized!

★ Willow, with a little bending and flexing to make it more supple, can be used to make baskets, nesting boxes and all sorts.

★ You can fire the seed heads of the plantain plant (a weed that grows all over the place) by picking them from the base of the stem, folding the stem over itself just below the head and pulling. The head will pop off and can go quite far!

★ Sticky weed (sometimes known as goose grass) will stick to woollen clothes really easily. Put some on your friend's back and see how long it takes before they notice.

★ Since moths are attracted to light, you can attract loads of them by shining a bright light on to a white sheet at night.

★ The methods that plants use to disperse their seeds include parachutes, gliders, helicopters and spinners. Sycamore seeds are the very best of nature's helicopters. See how many seeds you can find and work out how they disperse themselves.

MAKE YOUR OWN HAMMOCK

Time for an afternoon nap. What do you do? Make a hammock of course. It's really not that difficult but it will require a sense of balance, a sense of humour and an old double sheet or an old duvet cover. You might not get it exactly right first time. Just remember not to hang the hammock too high up the trees. That way, when you fall out of it later, you won't hurt yourself too much. Nobody wants to spend the last part of their weekend in A&E, do they?

Use either a double sheet folded in half lengthways for strength or a duvet cover. A single duvet cover might not be big enough for anyone but the kids.

Tie a big double knot in each corner. That will give you your basic hammock shape. Next get two pieces of rope – how long you need will depend on how far apart your trees are! Three metres (10 feet) or so should be enough. Tie one end of the rope to the sheet, just below one of the knots on the short side. Loop the rope around the tree twice (and above a branch to stop it slipping down) and then tie the other end just below the second knot on the short side of the sheet. Repeat with the other piece of rope at the other end of the sheet, but be careful not to stretch the fabric too tightly; you'll need some give in it. *Voila*!

Now you can have a go at getting in it. Don't blame me when it all goes wrong. It will. That's part of the fun.

250

MUSHROOM SEASON

For some people, like my neighbour Freddy the Farmer, mushroom season (around October to November) is a time for getting excited. Off he goes into the woods with the dogs, his basket and his wellies to his favourite mushroom spots in search of the highly prized ceps. If he's lucky he'll pick up a chicken of the woods too, and perhaps some field mushrooms.

Freddy knows what he's doing because he has been doing it forever. He knows where, when and what to look for. It's to be admired, all that knowledge and being at ease with the countryside. But it's not to say that we can't have our own share of the mushroom harvest. The thing to do is to have someone like Freddy show you the ropes and then swot up with a good field guide. If you're not sure what you're picking, then you shouldn't be picking it at all.

Strictly speaking, mushroom season is a bit of a misnomer as a lot of the more commonly foraged mushrooms can be found over the summer and autumn. The easiest to find and identify are field mushrooms, ceps, fairy-ring mushrooms and puffballs, which can all be picked from July to November.

FREDDY'S MILKY CHANTERELLES ON TOAST

Freddy loves his food. And he loves his chanterelles. So it seems only right to give him his due and tell you about this easy recipe. I promised not to tell where he took me picking but I didn't promise not to spill the beans about the way he likes to cook them. This he does in a pan with butter and garlic. He then adds a little milk and simmers the lot for about 20 minutes over a very low heat. The smell when it cooks is divine. The mushroom mix is served on white toast with a little salted butter. It has to be white bread and it has to be salted butter. The parsley garnish was for my benefit.

wild MUSHROOMS on toast

For the mushroom forager there is no greater treat than the taste of the first wild mushrooms of the season – a gift from nature. If it isn't your lucky day today and you haven't managed to find anything worth taking home, you can still make this with regular brown mushrooms instead.

FOR 1 FORAGER

KNOB OF BUTTER

2 HANDFULS WILD MUSHROOMS, SUCH AS GIROLLES OR CEPS (PORCINI), WIPED WITH
**   A DAMP CLOTH OR BRUSHED WITH A MUSHROOM BRUSH**

1 TSP OR SO FRESH THYME LEAVES (NICE BUT NOT ESSENTIAL)

2 TBSP CREAM

SQUEEZE OF LEMON JUICE

1 LARGE SLICE SOURDOUGH OR OTHER RUSTIC-STYLE BREAD WITH A GOOD CRUST,
**   TOASTED OR AS IT COMES**

Heat the butter in a frying pan. Halve or slice any large mushrooms. When the butter is sizzling, add the mushrooms and thyme and cook together for 7-8 minutes, tossing them around in the butter. Add the cream, lemon juice and some seasoning. Bubble together for a minute, then pile on to the bread and eat with a smile.

CHICKEN of the woods RISOTTO

Chicken of the woods is curiously, as the name suggests, very much like chicken in texture. Like many fungi it grows on old trees, particularly oak. It is best eaten when it is young and at its most colourful – bright yellows and oranges.

If you prefer, you can use ceps, brown field mushrooms or even the real thing, chicken. If you want to use chicken, just add 3 handfuls, cooked and shredded, towards the end of the cooking time for the rice, along with a little lemon zest.

FOR 4

 OLIVE OIL

1 ONION, FINELY CHOPPED

2 CLOVES GARLIC, FINELY CHOPPED

350ML (ABOUT 255G) RISOTTO RICE

SMALL TUMBLER OF WHITE WINE

1 LITRE HOT VEGETABLE STOCK (USE MUSHROOM STOCK CUBES IF YOU COME ACROSS THEM)

1 TBSP BUTTER, PLUS A KNOB TO FINISH

4 HANDFULS (ABOUT 250G) CHICKEN OF THE WOODS MUSHROOM, CLEANED AND SLICED
   THINLY, THEN CUT INTO SMALL PIECES

2 TBSP GRATED PARMESAN (OR PECORINO), PLUS EXTRA TO SPRINKLE

3 TBSP CHOPPED PARSLEY OR CHIVES

Heat 2 tablespoons of olive oil in a large pan. Add the onion and cook for 8-10 minutes or until softened, adding the garlic for the last few minutes. Tip in the rice and stir for a minute or so over the heat. Pour in the wine and bring to a simmer, then bubble until nearly all the wine has evaporated. Pour in half the stock and simmer, stirring all the time, until the stock has been absorbed, about 10 minutes. Stir in the rest of the stock and continue to cook for a further 8-10 minutes or until the rice is *al dente* tender.

Meanwhile, heat the tablespoon of butter in a frying pan and fry the mushrooms with some seasoning for 6-7 minutes, tossing them around in the butter and bubbling away until any liquid has evaporated. When the rice is ready, stir in the mushrooms, Parmesan, the knob of butter and the herbs. Season to taste and eat as soon as possible, in bowls, with extra Parmesan to sprinkle on top.

THE HEDGEROW HARVEST

September, and everyone goes out to enjoy blackberrying along the hedgerows. The world and his dog will be out there at the side of the road, foraging for the juiciest berries. A walking stick can be helpful to hook down the highest branches or to hold back the whippy, thorny stems. Who would turn down the prospect of apple and blackberry pie? As the weather begins to turn sour, a little natural sugar will sweeten any day. Put on your wellies, pack up the pac a mac and get out there.

September is a great time of the year to be in the country or by the sea. The water is at its warmest, the summer visitors have long gone and the hedgerows are bursting with interesting stuff to collect. The surfing fraternity takes off at this time of year to stretch out the summer for a few more weeks and cash in on powerful autumn surf. It's a well-travelled camper van route through France and Spain to Portugal, or even Morocco. For us, with the kids back in school, it's evenings and weekends only. Sunday afternoons are spent walking in the woods, along the coastal path and on the suddenly deserted beaches. Mussels are back on the menu. Surf abounds. All is right with the world. It's a time of plenty.

Thankfully, the ritual of the September blackberry harvest is one of those pastimes that will never be lost. We all know how to do it and we all love it. If only we could remember what else in the hedgerows can be eaten. But there really is an awful lot. Keep a couple of Ziploc bags in your coat pocket – you can use them if you find anything interesting worth taking home. On the next couple of pages I've set out of some of the easier things to recognise.

HAZELNUTS: Get in before the squirrels do. That's all I can say. It's all in the timing. These furry nut-terrorists are all over the hazel trees in September as they make ready for the winter ahead. It's no wonder. Hazelnuts are reported to have all sorts of magical health benefits, particularly when it comes to preventing heart disease and cancer. Like all stuff in the wild, the best hazelnuts are picked in the woods away from pollution and harmful chemicals.

Picking hazelnuts is a patient game and one that's been practised for centuries. Just wait until they are ripe enough...

ROSE HIPS: Rose hips, or haws, the fruit of the dog rose, have long been known for their high vitamin C content and their antioxidant properties. People use hips for all kinds of things. They may well be another of nature's quiet wonder foods. So if you see them in the wild don't hesitate to pick a few.

I use them to make tea, which is healthy and easy to make. Since the rose hips need to be dried first, pick a few when you see them and chuck them on the dashboard to dry out in the sun. Otherwise you might want to take them home – look at the method on page 264.

SLOES: Did anyone ever give you one of these as a child and try to convince you they taste lovely? You wouldn't forget eating these 1cm ($^1/_2$ inch) long, dark blue berries. Sloes should be treated with respect and never eaten raw or they'll suck the moisture from your mouth like a kitchen towel. The best time to pick sloes is after the first frost, but if you can't wait that long, take them home and pop them in the freezer overnight. The main reason to pick sloes is to make sloe gin. It's easily the best gin I have ever tried. To make it you need:

500G SLOES
200G CASTER SUGAR
1 LITRE GIN

First prick the sloes and put them in a large sterilised bottle or Kilner jar. Next add the sugar, then top up with gin. Seal the lid tightly. Leave the jar in a cool dark place. Shake the container every day for a month, then every week for another month. After that it's ready to enjoy.

Beware

Red Squirrels

ELDERBERRIES: Another easy-to-recognise treat that's fun to pick, and which you may want to take home with you. The berries appear from late August, earlier in some years. Remember to leave a few behind for the birds.

Elderberries are full of vitamin C so there is every reason to take a little time and make some elderberry cordial.

Put the elderberries in a stainless steel pan with enough water to cover, and boil for 10 minutes. Then crush and strain the berries to extract the juice. For every 570ml juice you are left with, add about 450g sugar. Add a few cloves for each 570ml liquid, then boil this mixture up for another 10 minutes. Add nutmeg to taste. Decant into bottles or screw-top jars. Use straight away or keep in the fridge for up to one month.

SUNDAY TEA

Once you've explored, picked, foraged and taken it easy, it's time to put the kettle on again and enjoy one last wild tea. And what better to have with it than a little something to remind us of the great times we just had? Got any of the rocky road left for the road? Thought not. But never mind. Dive into a cream tea or take a big bite out of one of Sarah's best-ever crab sandwiches instead.

Forager's SALAD with cheddar, APPLES and toasted NUTS

There are lots of wild salad leaves that are delicious in salads and well worth investigating. Use a reference book to check you can eat your treasured finds – *The Forager Handbook* by Miles Irving is excellent for foraging in Britain. Add a few edible flowers to the salad if you like – daisies are very pretty, as are dandelion petals if separated and sprinkled over – and honeysuckle is lovely to add too. This salad is perfect for autumn. If you want to make it more substantial, boil some new potatoes or Jerusalem artichokes till tender, then thickly slice and add. In the spring try swapping the cheddar for crumbled goat's cheese.

FOR 4

OLIVE OIL

4 HANDFULS SHELLED COB NUTS (OR HAZELNUTS), ROUGHLY CHOPPED

8 HANDFULS SMALL-TO-MEDIUM SALAD LEAVES/GREENERY, SUCH AS LAMB'S LETTUCE, CHICKWEED,
   BUCK'S-HORN PLANTAIN, HAIRY BITTER-CRESS, DOG VIOLET, FAT HEN, WILD ROCKET

2 HEADS CHICORY, LEAVES SEPARATED

4 HANDFULS MATURE CHEDDAR CHEESE SHAVINGS

2 DESSERT APPLES OR SMALL PEARS, CORED AND THINLY SLICED

FOR THE DRESSING

1 TSP RUNNY HONEY

2 TBSP OLIVE OIL

1 TBSP WALNUT OIL

1 TBSP RED OR WHITE WINE VINEGAR

PINCH OF ENGLISH MUSTARD POWDER (OPTIONAL)

Heat a little oil in a frying pan and when hot add the nuts, tossing them over the heat until golden. Meanwhile, toss all the other salad ingredients in a large bowl and make the dressing by mixing all the components together in a cup or jam jar.

Add the warm, toasted nuts to the salad along with the dressing, a couple of pinches of sea salt and some freshly milled black pepper. Toss everything thoroughly, then tip into 4 bowls.

Best-ever CRAB sandwiches

If you've had luck on your side and have found yourself a 'take home'-sized crab on your crabbing adventures then this is the way to have it. Otherwise, nip to the fishmonger's and get yourself a dressed crab. Either way, this is a luxurious treat.

FOR 2

SOFT UNSALTED BUTTER

4 LARGE FRESHLY CUT SLICES BROWN OR WHITE BREAD

4 TBSP BROWN CRABMEAT

4 TBSP WHITE CRABMEAT

4 TBSP MAYONNAISE

1 EATING APPLE, CORED AND CHOPPED SMALL

1 LEMON

PINCH OF CHILLI POWDER OR PAPRIKA

2 HANDFULS ROCKET OR WATERCRESS

Lightly butter the bread, then spread two of the slices with brown crabmeat. Mix the white crabmeat with the mayonnaise, apple, a squeeze of lemon juice, the chilli powder or paprika (or freshly ground black pepper) and a pinch of crushed sea salt. Spread the white crabmeat mixture on top of the brown crab meat. Then top with the rocket or watercress and put the lid on. Cut into quarters and devour.

Drop SCONES with quick raspberry JAM and CLOTTED CREAM

What good is a cup of tea on a Sunday afternoon in the country, without a scone? None at all, I'd say. And just because you're in the van, it doesn't mean you can't enjoy the heavenly pleasures of clotted cream, jam and scones. Sarah's quick jam has a much fresher flavour than your common-or-garden jam that comes in jars. If you've been to the pick-your-own then why not make-your-own? Indeed.

MAKES ABOUT 16

FOR THE QUICK RASPBERRY JAM AND CREAM

 3 MUGFULS (ABOUT 400G) RASPBERRIES

¾ MUGFUL (ABOUT 150G) CASTER SUGAR

BIG BOWL OF CLOTTED CREAM, TO SERVE

FOR THE DROP SCONES

1¹/₂ MUGFULS (ABOUT 225G) SELF-RAISING FLOUR

1 TSP BAKING POWDER

2 TBSP CASTER SUGAR

200ML MILK

2 LARGE EGGS

BUTTER AND OIL, FOR FRYING

For the jam, tip the raspberries into a medium-sized pan with the sugar and place over a low heat. Slowly heat the fruit and sugar, stirring to dissolve the sugar as you do so and squashing the raspberries with the back of the spoon. Once all the fruit has collapsed and you are left with a seedy liquid with a few lumps and bumps – after 10 to 15 minutes – increase the heat and bring to the boil. Boil the jam vigorously for 8 minutes, giving it a stir from time to time. The fruit will take on a jammy aroma and will thicken. Take the pan off the heat and leave the jam to cool a little – it will thicken further as it cools. Tip into a heat-proof bowl and leave to cool completely.

   To make the scones, sieve the flour and baking powder into a bowl and stir in the sugar and a pinch of salt. Make a well in middle. Lightly beat the milk with the eggs in a jug and pour the liquid into the well, then whisk the liquid into the flour – a balloon whisk is ideal for this. Once all the liquid has been incorporated, you should have a smooth, thickish mixture.

Heat a tablespoon of oil and a small knob of butter together in a frying pan and, when sizzling, add 1 tablespoon of mixture for each scone. You should be able to cook 4 or 5 at a time, keeping them spaced apart in the pan. As soon as bubbles appear on the surface of the scones, the undersides should be golden – 2 to 3 minutes – so flip them and cook the other side for the same amount of time. Continue until all the mixture is used up, adding more oil and butter before cooking each batch, as needed. Eat barely warm, each one topped with raspberry jam and clotted cream.

A DIFFERENT KIND OF BREW

✳ Who said tea had to be made with tea leaves? Not us. Making tisanes and herbal teas from things you have found or from other unexpected ingredients is great fun and highly satisfying. Why not? Here are a few to try.

YARROW: Can be found most of the year. It comes from the same family as chamomile and is easy to spot. The leaves make a lovely, slightly savoury herbal tea and can be used fresh (or dried). Put a handful of fresh, slightly bruised yarrow heads into a teapot and top up with boiling water. Leave to infuse before pouring. Chamomile flower heads can be used in the same way – you will find them in the summer months.

WILD MINT: Mint comes in different types depending on the habitat. Use your foraging guide to help you locate them. You can make a refreshing pick-me-up herbal tisane in the same way as you would with yarrow. Sweeten with honey to taste. Wild mint is also lovely to add to summer salads.

ROSE HIPS: Can be foraged from late summer but they need to be dried before using. Pick a bag of rose hips, spread them out and leave them to dry and shrivel slightly. This usually takes a week or so, possibly less on a sunny windowsill. After this, cut the rose hips in half and remove the seeds and hairy centres – these can make your hands itch so try not to touch them too much. Spread the halved hips out and leave to dry completely, another week or so.

    To use, gently simmer a tablespoonful in a mugful of water for 15-20 minutes, sweeten to taste. Rose hips are full of vitamin C so avoid using an aluminium pan as it will take away the goodness.

ROOT GINGER: Peel a thumb-sized piece and slice into discs. Put a few discs in each cup, add a squeeze of lemon and top up with boiling water. Leave to infuse for a couple of minutes before sipping.

LEMONGRASS: Chop and add a few pieces to each cup. Top up with boiling water and leave to infuse as above. It is lovely mixed with ginger or a small sprig of rosemary.

PACKING UP AND SHIPPING OUT

If you really can't manage to stay another day (maybe you need a better excuse, see page 268) then you'll have to face up to the fact that you're going to have to pack up. This is the time to scratch your head. Most campers will do it at some point. It involves standing in a field surrounded by all your possessions, wondering how on earth you're going to fit them all back in to the van.

A methodical approach works best. Sending the rest of the team off to have some fun also works for me. That way I can only get annoyed with myself when I have to pack and repack until it all fits in to my liking.

The first thing to do is get all your recycling done. While it might seem like a pain to do when you're in a field, it's still just as important as it is at home. Most discerning campsites will have recycling facilities so please use them if they're available. Next, if you can, give away any food that you don't want to take with you but which will only go to waste if you don't.

Third, do the washing-up. I know it's tempting to take it home but do it on site and you'll have less to do once you are at home. The more you pack up the van as if you're going away again, the less you'll have to sort out next time.

Finally, once it's all in, do a final check. Have a quick scout around your bit of the campsite. You're bound to realise you've still got the electric plugged in, or stub your toe on a missing peg. And you'll be able to spot any last-minute bits of rubbish. If you have left the campsite exactly as you found it then you should be a very happy camper indeed.

You can come again

CAMPER VAN LAW

Cricket wouldn't be cricket without the rules of cricket, would it? So why should camper van living be any different? Maybe it's just not important enough to warrant a code of conduct or a manifesto, but there must be rules or we will all live in chaos. So, in the absence of such a list I have created my own. It's my own set of values of course and, as such, much of it is based on blind prejudice and the fact that I own a T25. But it's designed to help us all live in perfect harmony. Let me know how you get on with it.

One tribe, united by our love of camper van living. All together now...

★ First up prepares the first brew of the day. No exceptions.

★ One up, all up.

★ Last one in the sea is a sissy.

★ It's ok to wave at vans that are newer than your own.

★ Always wave back at vans that have waved to you.

★ You will spend time with your roadside assistance provider. Get used to it.

★ Check the oil. Check it again. And again. You get the picture.

★ If the oil light or the battery light comes on, STOP immediately.

★ No top boxes. Not ever.

★ No caravans.

★ Take wellingtons.

★ Pack the van yourself if you want to find anything.

★ Take your litter home.

★ You can't go camping and not have a burger. See page 156 for details.

★ Go and have some fun.

MISSING YOU

Have you had a great weekend? Then you might want to stay another day. Why bother breaking your neck to get back on time? Put it off, make hay, the sun is shining. Who needs a job anyway?

The 10 best excuses for not making it in to work on Monday morning

★ My van broke down and I am four hundred miles away waiting for parts to be imported from Europe / Brazil. I'll be back in a week / month.

★ The wind changed. It's going to take me longer to get back than I thought.

★ We're stranded on an island. The weather's taken a turn for the worse and the ferry isn't coming for another four days. I'll be in next Monday.

★ I am at the end of the rainbow. It's nice. I think I'll stay a while.

★ I found a hundred cases of whisky on a remote beach and I am waiting for the Receiver of the Wreck to bring me a salvage form. There's a case in it for you.

★ My kids have buried me in the sand. Please call the coastguard as the tide is rising fast.

★ I'll be there as soon as the bull lets us out of the field.

★ We're selling up and moving to Hastings / Whitby / Whitstable…

★ I met someone.

★ I've got a job in a surf shack. I resign.

LISTINGS

VW CAMPER VAN HIRE COMPANIES (UK AND IRELAND)

SOUTH EAST

VW Camper Hire
Enfield, Middlesex
www.vwcamper-hire.com

East Coast Campers
Canvey Island, Essex
www.eastcoastcampers.co.uk

Snail Trail Ltd
Bedfordshire
www.snailtrail.co.uk

My VW Campervan
Milton Keynes, Bucks.
www.myvwcampervan.com

Vanilla Splits Ltd
West Sussex
www.vanillasplits.com

VDub Campers Ltd
West Sussex
www.vdubcampers.co.uk

Go Campers
Kent
www.gocampers.co.uk

SOUTH

Campervan Rental
Dorset
www.campervanrental.co.uk

South Coast Campers
Dorset
www.southcoastcampers.com

Comfy Campers
Cheltenham, Gloucs.
www.comfycampers.co.uk

Isle of Wight Camper Van Holidays
Shanklin
www.isleofwightcampers.co.uk

SOUTH WEST

O'Connors Campers
Okehampton, Devon
www.oconnorscampers.co.uk

Classic Camper Van Hire
www.classiccampervanhire.co.uk

Devon Classic Campers
www.devonclassiccampers.co.uk

South West Camper Hire
Exeter, Devon
www.southwestcamperhire.com

Devon Happy Campers
Honiton, Devon
www.devonhappycampers.co.uk

MIDLANDS

Camper 4 Hire
Leicestershire
www.camper4hire.co.uk

Cool Campervans
Derby
www.coolcampervans.com

Outer Motive
Warwick
www.outermotive.co.uk

NORTH

Liberty Campers
West Yorkshire
www.libertycampers.co.uk

Lakeland Campers
Cumbria
www.lakelandcampers.co.uk

Classic Campers Ltd
Carlisle, Cumbria
www.classiccampers.co.uk

Easy Hire Motorhomes Ltd
Manchester, Lancashire
www.easyhiremotorhomes.co.uk

SCOTLAND

Happy Highland Campers
Dingwall, Highlands
www.happyhighlandcampers.co.uk

IRELAND

Lazydays
Wicklow
www.lazydays.ie

Retro Rentals
Co. Wicklow
www.retrorentals.ie

MECHANICS AND SERVICING

Got an emergency situation? Get on the blower.

SOUTH EAST

Jack's Garage
London W10
020 7243 8926

Tony Hines Autos
Wallington, Surrey
020 8647 8329

Westside Motors
Woodford Green, Essex
020 8505 5215

Wolfsburg Performance Services
Chertsey, Surrey
01932 701521

VDub Campers Ltd
West Sussex
07929 366429

SOUTH

VW Camper Company Limited
Oxfordshire
01295 812266

G'Day Kombis
Oxfordshire
01865 400884

VW City Portsmouth
Hampshire
02392 293345

VW Camper Expert
Dorset
07801 548128

SOUTH WEST

South West Classic VWs
South Molton, Devon
01769 573020

MAD Workshop
Avon
01179 352200

MIDLANDS

Outermotive
Warwick
01926 408942

NORTH

Volkstech
Morecambe, Lancs.
01524 843383

Wolfsburg VW
www.wolfsburgvw.com
Chorley, Lancashire
01254 830432

Brickwerks
Holmfirth, Yorkshire
01484 664017

IRELAND

Krazykombis
Kilkenny
086 314 6412

Ireland Air-Cooled Centre
Armagh
02 837 998188 or
02 837 548072

Cosy Classics
Dublin
01 4418759

CAMPSITES

How could we ever do anything more than scratch the surface here? These are some of the sites that we have visited and loved, or that our friends have recommended. Some top places to visit if you're pootling about in the area.

SOUTH

Hurley Riverside Park
Hurley, Oxfordshire
01628 824493
www.hurleyriversidepark.co.uk

Greenway Farm Caravan and Camping Park
Forest of Dean, Gloucestershire
01594 544877
www.greenwayfarm.org

SOUTH WEST

Batcombe Vale Campsite
Somerset
01749 831207
www.batcombevale.co.uk

Stoke Barton Farm
Hartland Quay, North Devon
01237 441238
www.westcountry-camping.co.uk

River Dart Country Park
Ashburton, South Devon
01364 652511
www.riverdart.co.uk

Treen Farm Campsite
Treen, Cornwall
Tel: 01736 810273
www.treenfarmcampsite.co.uk

Ayr Holiday Park
St Ives, Cornwall
www.ayrholidaypark.co.uk

Bryder Farm Campsite
Bude, Cornwall
01288 355382

NORTH

Eskdale Camping and Caravanning Club Site
Cumbria
01946 723253
www.campingandcaravanning-club.co.uk

Knight Stainforth Hall Camping and Caravanning Park
Settle, North Yorkshire
01729 822200
www.knightstainforth.co.uk

The Quiet Site
Cumbria
07768 727016
www.thequietsite.co.uk

WALES

Nant-y-Big Beachside Holidays
Porth Ceiriad, North Wales
01758 712686
www.nantybig.co.uk

SCOTLAND

Camusdarach Campsite
Nr Arisaig, Highlands
01687 450221
www.road-to-the-isles.org.uk/camusdarach-campsite.html

IRELAND

Wave Crest Campsite
Caherdaniel, Co. Kerry
www.wavecrestcamping.com

LISTINGS

VW SHOWS AND EVENTS

There are lots of meets, swaps and shows all over the place that could keep you busy all weekend, every weekend. Here's a selection:

FEBRUARY

Dub Freeze
Bingley Hall, Staffordshire
www.dubfreeze.co.uk

MARCH

Volksworld Show
Esher, Surrey
www.volksworld.com

MAY

Stonor Park
Henley-on-Thames, Oxfordshire
www.essexveedubbers.org.uk

Volks Fling
Biggar, Scotland
www.volksfling.co.uk

All Types VW Show
Bodelwyddan Castle, Wales
www.alltypesvwshow.co.uk

Run to the Sun
Newquay, Cornwall
www.runtothesun.co.uk

Van Jamboree
Newark, Nottinghamshire
www.vanjamboree.co.uk

Van West
Nr Yeovil, Somerset
www.vanwest.net

JUNE

The Bus Stop Over
Wymeswold, Leicestershire
www.thebusstopover.com

Bristol Volksfest
Wraxall, Somerset
www.bristolvolksfest.co.uk

JULY

London Volksfest
Harlow, Essex
www.vwaction.co.uk

Dubstock
Madley, Hertfordshire
www.dubstock.co.uk

AUGUST

Dubs at the beach
Paignton, Devon

Cornwall VWOC Jamboree
Stithians, Cornwall
www.cvwoc.co.uk

Gathering Off The Hill (GOTH)
Croston, Lancashire
www.volkswigan.co.uk

Run to the hills
Derbyshire
www.runtothehills.org.uk

VW Northwest
Nr Knutsford, Cheshire
www.vwnw.co.uk

Volksfest Wales
Port Talbot, South Wales
www.volksfestwales.org.uk

SEPTEMBER

Vanfest
Malvern, Worcestershire
www.vanfest.org

VW Action
Santa Pod Raceway,
Wellingborough, Northants.
www.vwaction.co.uk

OCTOBER

Brighton Breeze
Split Screen Van Club Cruise
to Brighton
www.ssvc.org.uk

**North Devon VW Club
Final Fling**
Woolacombe, Devon
www.northdevonvwclub.co.uk

**Scottish Volkswagen
Owners Festival**
Bathgate, Scotland
www.svwof.co.uk

NOVEMBER

Busfreeze
Staffordshire
www.busfreeze.co.uk

FESTIVALS

Looking for a festival? There are literally hundreds of them to shake your booty at. This list is just a handful of the more unusual festivals available. For more details, ask the Google.

SOUTH EAST

Wood, Wallingford, *May*
Music and nature get equal billing at this family-friendly, ecotastic acoustic festival. Make stuff, learn about wood, have a great time, listen to great music. Whittler's delight.

Cambridge Folk Festival, Cherry Hinton Hall, *July*
More folk music. Attracts 10,000 attendees every year and showcases a diverse mix of folk artists in a relaxed and family-friendly atmosphere.

SOUTH WEST

Gold Coast Oceanfest, Croyde, *July*
We dig this festival because it's friendly and has a genuine conscience. Beach and ocean sports events sit side by side with great music. All with an eco-message. If you love the beach this is the one for you.

Sunrise Celebration, Shepton Mallet, *June* .
Sunrise Celebration is an ethical living and music festival that's committed to sustainability. Music, solar-powered cinema, healing stalls, eco-fashion stalls, kids' areas and educational activities. Come on down.

MIDLANDS

Ledbury Poetry Festival, *July*
Off the pages and into the open at this, the UK's largest celebration of verse. 'Jazz poetry' sounds intriguing, if not a bit bonkers. Zealous? Get your beret ready and head for Ledbury.

Bloodstock Open Air, Walton-upon-Trent, *August*
For those about to rock. There will be blood, there will be metal, you can guarantee it. 9,000 metalheads will turn up and headbang their way through some truly hardcore rock. Love it!

NORTH

Kendal Calling, Penrith, *July*
Snow? In Cumbria? In the middle of summer? It's a possibility but it'll only be a certainty at Kendall Calling. There is a snow beach, tobogganing, snow bars and all sorts. Well I never. Oh yes and some indie bands and lots of stuff for kids too.

Solfest, Cumbria, *August*
Family-friendly festival with a fab atmosphere. Get there early or you'll have to park on a slope. Mind you, we don't care. It's a big party with compulsory fancy dress and lots of great activities for kids. Ours loved it, yours will too.

Whitby Folk Week, *August*
The UK's biggest traditional folk event with the best fish and chips in the northern hemisphere right on site too (so they say). Real live folk music, all week.

WALES

Wakestock, Abersoch, *July*
Wakestock is the main event in the wakeboarding calendar and anyone who's anyone will be heading here to compete and get down to some funky music. Excellent.

Green Man Festival, Brecon Beacons, *August*
A popular ethically-minded festival in a brilliant setting. Literature, film, comedy and all-night bonfires are all part of the festival's unique identity.

SCOTLAND

Rockness, Dores, *June*
Monsters may or may not lurk near the festival site. Who knows? But it's got to be worth a peek, hasn't it?

Wickerman Festival, Dumfries and Galloway, *July*
A mini-Glasto with an eclectic range of music and family-oriented fun. At midnight on the Saturday a 30ft wickerman gets torched. Wooooo!

IRELAND

Cat Laughs Festival, Kilkenny, *June*
It's all about the laughing at this festival that celebrates the art of comedy. You just know it's going to be very random, don't you? All sorts of wonderful nonsense.

RECIPE INDEX

RECIPE INDEX

ACKNOWLEDGEMENTS

FROM MARTIN...

Oops! I feel a Gwyneth coming on. Hardly surprising really. There's a lot to be thankful for. Everyone should try mucking about in a camper, even just for a weekend. For me, the whole thing has been made possible and infinitely better by the following people:

Elizabeth Hallett, editor and believer.
Sarah, chief foodie with unfailingly delicious ideas. Brilliant.
Joanne, the long suffering trouble and strife, who came along for the ride, whatever the weather.
Maggie and Charlie, the dustbins, for making us laugh.
Damian Horner, a man who also likes adventures in small spaces, for his timely introductions. A thousand thanks.
Martin and Cath, who kept the faith, lent me their children and polished their van. Still rocking after all these years.
Thomas and Jack, for being the new generation of camper van heroes.
John Kinton and Phil Taylor, who moved me with the lumbering dignity of their beautiful aged Westfalia Splitties. Cover girls.
Ian Marchant at South West Classic VWs for his mechanical opinions and expertise.
Richard Woods at Just Kampers for lending us some fabulous camping accessories.
Simon and Joel Cooper, champion shrimpers.
Abi, Nico, Alfie, Rosie and Nick, the original WST, for actually doing it. Thanks for the inspiration.
Sean McKay, freaky eater and very good friend, whose famously odd tastes deserve a mention. Just don't make me eat goose barnacles again, no matter how tasty they are.
Stefan and Georgia, for a fab day on the beach eating limpets.
The Devon and Cornwall Constabulary, for the bad news about driving in flip flops. Cheers.
Everyone with odd sandwich choices. You guys are wrong 'uns.
Sean Corin at Northam Burrows Country Park and Torridge District Council for allowing us to use the old dump road to shoot the cover. Some dump eh?

Justin Seedhouse from The National Trust for allowing access to the loveliest beach in the world.

Paul and Christine Smale, for passing on their knowledge, however unwittingly, over a few pints. And yes! It was a crawfish.

Cai, for giving us the Bude Surf Report (AKA The Daily Chuckle) and for telling us when to go and when not to go.

The Adventure Babies, for their music and friendship.

Jason at Danbury Motor Caravans.

Jamie Harper, new Copy Monkey, for researching Festivals and Events.

Zoe, Sam and Pete at O'Connors Campers.

Mary Maxwell at the DfT.

Andy Clarke at www.ukmotorhomes.net

Emma Bridgewater for the loan of tins, plates and bowls.

Everyone at Saltyard Books – Al, Bill, Bryony, Camilla, Claire, James, Jason, Katie, Katy, Sarah...

...and Frank Blundell, who cut bars of soap in half, made kites, painted pictures, wrote poetry and quietly, in his own way, showed us the righteous path.

...but finally Sister Kate, Charlotte, Charlie, Jamie, Sam and all the staff of ward 34 for giving Maggie back to us when we thought all was lost.

...AND FROM SARAH

Thank you to friends and family, who sipped and munched their way through the recipes and gave their honest, treasured opinions along the way.

PHOTOGRAPHY

Most of the photographs in this book were taken by Martin Dorey.
Food photography and cover photography by Dan Jones.
Additional photography supplied by Dave Keightley (howaboutdave.com),
Nico Chapman (www.nicochapman.blogspot.com), Martin Knight, Joanne Dorey,
TYF Adventures (www.tyf.com), O'Connors Campers (www.oconnorscampers.co.uk),
Guy Harrop (www.guyharrop.com) and Simon Mitchell (www.corduroylines.co.uk).

First published in Great Britain in 2010 by Saltyard Books
An imprint of Hodder & Stoughton
An Hachette UK company

4

Text © Martin Dorey 2010
Recipes marked with ✳ © Sarah Randell 2010
Recipes marked with ⇥ © Martin Dorey 2010

Photography © Martin Dorey 2010

Photographs on pages:
ii, 18, 20, 24, 52, 68, 105, 109, 113, 117, 135,
137, 143, 163, 164, 168, 178, 185, 227, 230,
235, 236, 258, 260, 263 and 279 © Dan Jones 2010
202 and 203 © Dave Keightley 2010
193 (top) and 199 © Nico Chapman 2010
246 and 247 © Martin Knight 2010
206 and 209 © TYF Adventures 2010
270 © O'Connors Campers 2010
14 and 33 © Guy Harrop 2010
208 and 209 © Simon Mitchell 2010

A CIP catalogue record for this title is available from the British Library.

ISBN 978 1 444 703 89 4

Design and page make-up by Craig Burgess
Copy editor Jo Hill
Indexer Caroline Wilding

Typeset in Rotis serif and Avenir

Printed and bound by Butler Tanner & Dennis Ltd, Frome and London

Mixed Sources
Product group from well-managed
forests, and other controlled sources
www.fsc.org Cert no. SGS-COC-002987
© 1996 Forest Stewardship Council
FSC

Saltyard Books
338 Euston Road
London NW1 3BH

www.saltyardbooks.co.uk